The clue of the bla

M. Thiriet has been per

by the promise of a new

trick. Bobby Thiriet and

the tricksters and recover

always confronted by the elusive black cat. However their persistence pays off, helped by the Puisay Students' News *and its willing readers.*

Paul Berna

The clue of the black cat

Translated from the French by John Buchanan-Brown
Illustrated by Prudence Seward

KNIGHT BOOKS

the paperback division of Brockhampton Press

SBN 340 03985 X

This edition first published 1970 byKnight Books, the paperback division of Brockhampton Press Ltd, Leicester

Printed and bound in Great Britain by Cox & Wyman Ltd, London, Reading and Fakenham

First published in 1963 by Société Nouvelle des Editions, G.P., as Le témoignage du chat noir
First published in Great Britain by The Bodley Head Ltd, 1964

Contents

I

The bowels of the earth – Rue Mirandole

At four-fifteen, out came the last swarm of day boys through the south gate into the Rue Pochet. Bobby elbowed his way out of the scrum to stand sensibly aside. In a matter of seconds his class-mates had scattered from around him like a flock of sparrows. The November dusk was drawing in: the school caretaker in his white overall was impatiently shaking his bunch of keys before closing the gate with a grumble at the slow-coaches. Bobby waited on the empty pavement for a moment, as in the school the lights went out one by one in the vast windows overlooking the street. It grew darker and darker.

Up the Avenue de Paris strode George Thiriet. Turning the corner by the school he spotted at once the slim shape standing by the gate – a mop of fair hair enabled him to recognize his youngest son at a distance. As he approached, George tried to smile, but although the brim of his hat was pulled well down, it could not hide the wretched expression on his face.

'Hi! Bobby!' he called cheerfully. 'Guess what happened?'

Bobby shrugged.

'It all fell through,' he said unemotionally. 'As usual . . .'

George hugged his son clumsily to hide his embarrassment.

'Five-room luxury flat for sale in a skyscraper on the Place Brémontier,' he explained bitterly. 'Had to put down half the price in cash. Anyway it was too dear for us. And too grand – we've no business living above our means!'

Slowly they moved off towards the Avenue de Paris. The street lights had come on as if by magic and all around them sprang the new town, its white buildings glistening against a lowering, foggy sky.

George rested his left hand on his son's shoulder and his spirits rose in the aura of affection this contact aroused.

'Why don't we move to the other side of Paris?' Bobby suddenly suggested. 'Only the other day Mummy was saying that it's much easier to find somewhere to live in the northern suburbs.'

His father shook his head.

'We're stuck here because of my job, and your mother's, and your sister Belle's,' he said patiently. 'And that's not considering the rest of you. You boys have places in a good school. If we moved, the whole family would be seriously upset. And what would we gain? Sit down every night, tired out, in a chilly room to a scratch meal? No. We're better off sticking it out in Puisay waiting for something to turn up. After all, it isn't such a bad place.'

'Of course it isn't,' Bobby agreed sarcastically. 'But not everyone lives in the bowels of the earth – Rue Mirandole.'

They laughed. Then George sighed once more.

'I'm afraid it looks as though we're going to spend another Christmas there – our fifth!'

'Don't worry about me,' Bobby said coldly. 'All the sunlight my home ever sees comes through a crack in the ventilators.'

His father did not speak for a moment. He was really upset. They were at the traffic lights waiting to cross the Avenue down which poured an ever-thickening stream of cars as the evening drew on.

George looked at his watch.

'I'll take you to Fred's this time. He's the best barber in Puisay. I'm not going to have your hair butchered like it was last month.'

'I could have gone by myself,' Bobby protested.

'I need a bit of a trim, too. Anyway I promised you we'd go together.'

Beyond the new blocks, they were in the old part of Puisay – narrow streets rutted by the ceaseless passing of heavy lorries and lit by the glare from factory buildings. Beyond was the gaping void of the motorway, a dull rumble of traffic, and in the background brick and concrete and tall factory chimneys stretching to the horizon.

When they reached Fred's in the Place des Ormeaux, only one chair in the gentlemen's saloon was free.

'After you,' said George Thiriet as he helped his son in to it. 'Monsieur Basile is going to get to grips with that thicket of yours. When he's finished with you, you won't know yourself.'

All heads were turned in kindly notice of the over-awed little boy.

'A comic?' Monsieur Basile suggested as he adjusted the sheet.

'No thank you,' Bobby answered politely, 'I've got my paper.'

And out of his pocket he pulled four scanty pages of print, with a heading that made his neighbours goggle – *P.S.N.* The assistant got down to work. Itching with curiosity he could not keep his eyes off the paper. After a minute or two he asked, 'Whatever is the *P.S.N.*?'

'The *Puisay Students' News*,' Bobby translated. 'It's a newspaper written and produced by the boys at the Lycée Alfred-Jarry. The first issues had the full title, but then the chief editor decided to keep just the initials. *P.S.N.* sounds better, and it's got more punch, don't you think?'

His neighbours nodded.

'Anyway,' Bobby added, 'that doubled the circulation in a week.'

The prosperous old gentleman on his right could only have been cherishing faded hopes. The busy scissors barely skimmed the scanty halo of white hair round his bald crown.

'Anything interesting in that rag of yours?' he asked mockingly.

Bobby chose his words carefully.

'The *P.S.N.* just reports school life. There are three thousand of us in that barn of a place and you can't get to know everyone. So the *P.S.N.* helps us to keep in touch. Anyone can write what they like about anything – even if it's offering a second-hand transistor in part-exchange for a guitar.'

His left-hand neighbour was a tall individual with a long face split by a black moustache. He began to laugh as he bent his head to the finishing touch of the razor on the back of the neck.

'And how much does your *P.S.N.* cost?'

'It varies,' Bobby answered. 'Twenty-five to fifty centimes. Depends how much it costs to produce, but you always get your money's worth.'

The man with the moustache reached out a hand.

'Can I have a look at this wonderful rag of yours?' he inquired, pleasantly enough.

Bobby carefully folded and refolded his 'rag' and slipped it into his pocket.

'The *P.S.N.* is not for grown-ups,' he announced, to a gale of mirth.

The three customers at the other side of the saloon had their backs to him but the mirrors reflected their faces crystal clear under the strip lighting. To his left, next to the cash desk, was a venerable old gentleman with a beard and a pair of shrewd little eyes twinkling below bushy white brows. In the middle, right behind Bobby, a fair, clean-shaven man of about forty was having a trim; his crew-cut hair stuck up straight like hedgehog prickles. He did not talk and his half-closed eyes and expressionless face suggested a nonchalance that bordered on disdain. Finally, to the right was a fat, red-faced man with the unstoppable flow of talk of a cheapjack; even the douche of the shampoo could not silence him. George Thiriet, meanwhile, sat on the bench at the far end of the saloon awaiting his turn. It was pleasantly warm in there and the atmosphere was conducive to conversation. It was equally pleasant to hear the nice things said about his son.

'Only eleven?' the red-faced man said in amazement. 'I'd have given him a good two years more. It's frightening the way kids these days just shoot up.'

'You should see his older brothers,' George answered contentedly. 'A couple of young thugs! And then there's my eldest, a girl, she's a good head higher than her mother already!'

'I raise my hat to you,' the old man with the beard said pleasantly. 'You've got a job on your hands to feed and clothe that lot.'

'Oh, I get by,' George acknowledged. 'But it's a struggle all the same. The trouble is that the children suffer too.'

'What do they go without?' asked the red-faced man.

'A roof over their heads!'

A sudden hush fell upon the barber's shop and the six assistants stopped their snipping and turned towards the vagrant as one man.

'It's not really as bad as that,' George went on. 'We're not sleeping out in the street yet, but we're hardly much better off.'

He stopped. The owner, Monsieur Fred, had just finished with his customer, the tall, swarthy horse-faced man. The latter was putting on his overcoat before paying and leaving with a courteous good night to them all. Bobby winked an acknowledgement, his father got up at once to fill the empty chair, and the conversation resumed.

'Smell anything funny?' Monsieur Fred asked as he draped the sheet round George Thiriet.

The latter sniffed but could only smell hair-cream and lotion.

'Why do you ask?'

'That was Monsiur Sinet, the new police-chief of Puisay, who was in your chair a moment ago!'

'It makes no odds to me,' George retorted frankly.

There was a laugh. The balding man at the end of the row twisted his head to have a good look at Bobby's father. The latter was not forty yet, but his pallid, drawn face was care-worn and hardly improved by a pair of thick-lensed glasses.

'I'll bet you live in one of those disgraceful tenements in the Rue Mirandole?' he suggested sympathetically.

'The oldest and the most dilapidated,' George explained, 'the one on the corner of the Rue du Général-Tuboeuf.'

'What floor?'

'None. In the basement, more or less. It used to be the ground floor but the motorway embankment shuts all the light out of the windows. There are the six of us living in two tiny rooms. We have to use every inch of space and when we're all at home it's like an underground train in the rush hour. If anyone wants to come in or go out, or even move, everyone else is upset. Sometimes you only need to open a door carelessly to produce chaos!'

Monsieur Basile paused over Bobby's mop of hair in mild disbelief.

'Go on . . . you're exaggerating a bit aren't you?'

'I promise you I'm not,' George assured him. 'Ask the lad if you like.'

'Everything folds up in our home once we've finished with it,' Bobby said cheerfully. 'It has to if we're to move around – beds, chairs, tables, even the wash basin – unless Mummy's put some washing in to soak.'

'Bobby!' his father said reproachfully. 'Don't make things sound worse than they are.'

Everyone laughed except the fair clean-shaven man. He had his head in a basin while the shampoo was rinsed out of his spiky hair.

'Look around,' said the bearded man from his corner. 'You'll find something sooner or later.'

'But what a price!' George Thiriet sighed. 'For the last five years I've been doing all I can to get us out of this rat-hole. Every spare moment's been spent rushing round and never getting anywhere. I can't think of buying on mortgage. I don't want to tie up my salary, my wife's salary and my daughter's for the next fifteen to twenty years. Of course I could rent a nice four-roomed flat in one of the blocks on the Boulevard Champaubert. But it's the same there as anywhere else – apart from the high rent there's the key-money to take every penny I've set aside. A butcher or a grocer wouldn't take long to put the ten thousand francs back in the till, but that's five years' savings for an ordinary engineer in the Prochimac works.'

'What are you grumbling about?' someone behind him sniggered. 'Get out of your factory and open a shop.'

It was the red-faced man and his rudeness chilled the atmosphere of the barber's shop. Bobby lowered his head in embarrassment. Monsieur Fred and his assistants might be good for a gossip, but his father was wrong to let everyone know his troubles.

'Who is he?' George whispered, nodding towards red-face.

'He owns the biggest butcher's shop in Puisay, as it happens,' Monsieur Fred answered with a half-smile.

From then on conversation died down and the barbers busied themselves in silence. The first to leave, one after the other, were red-face and the man with the beard. Almost at once their places were taken by two quiet shy gentlemen. Bobby left his seat at the same time as the sleepy man with the spiky hair. The latter swept out without so much as a 'Good night'. At last when Monsieur Fred had released his victim, father and son went out into the foggy night air, each telling the other how smart he looked.

George Thiriet glanced at his watch. It was scarcely six o'clock and the gloomy Rue Mirandole was a stone's throw away.

'Let's take a stroll round town to blow the cobwebs away,' he said to Bobby. 'We'll do some window-shopping in the Avenue de Paris on our way back.'

Bobby couldn't have been better pleased. As they turned they almost bumped into the sleepy gentleman from the hairdresser's, the man Bobby had already begun to call the White Hedgehog in his own mind. The latter was wideawake now as he scrutinized, with a pair of laughing inquisitive eyes, the little engineer from the Prochimac and his son.

'I couldn't help overhearing what you were saying in the hairdresser's,' he told George. 'I expect you're thinking it's none of my business, but your difficulties really upset me.'

He spoke with deep sincerity and his eyes shone with goodwill. Bobby was most impressed by his plumpness, his expensive overcoat, dark blue Melton, and by the smart black hat which now hid his spiky hair. His whole being breathed an air of solid worth which commanded respect. George Thiriet for his part remained on the alert.

'I can see what's coming,' he said, screwing up a smile. 'You're going to produce a flat for me from out of your sleeve. You're not the first one, and I know the disappointment that's in store for me tonight or tomorrow.'

All the same there was no point in letting slip the slightest opportunity, and the stranger's self-assurance was catching. Bobby's elbow came up quietly to nudge his father encouragingly, as much as to say, 'Go on! What's the risk?'

The good-natured gentleman went straight to the point.

'Do you know the Belloy Private Estate, on the edge of the Parc de Sceaux?'

Bobby's eyes opened wide.

'We sometimes wander up there on a Sunday afternoon,' his father answered wearily. 'It's a mirage for people like us. Anyway I haven't changed my mind in the last few minutes. I cannot and I will not buy, even though there are any number of ways a man in a low-income group, as I am, can borrow money.'

'I understood that plainly enough,' the man said, without the slightest sign of impatience, 'but my mention of the Belloy Private Estate isn't just a suggestion out of the blue. Two-thirds of the money for that vast building project was put up by Metropolitan Properties. The Company retained forty leasehold flats and these are let at a very reasonable rent . . . Did you realize that?'

'No, I didn't,' the astonished George admitted.

'A four-roomed luxury flat works out at five or six hundred francs a month. That's not excessive for a family where both husband and wife are earning.'

George stared ahead, and as he calculated he let himself be tempted. They could manage. It would mean putting off the purchase of a car and they would have to cut down their holiday expenses.

'All the same, one of those flats has got to become vacant pretty quickly,' he said in a stumbling voice. 'We might just as well give up the whole idea now, if we've got to wait for ages.'

'Before the end of the week,' the stranger declared, 'your dream flat will be vacant in Block 6 on the Belloy Private Estate. And a very nice flat it is, too: I know it. The present tenant is a middle-aged lady. She had the misfortune to lose her husband last summer and since then her one idea has been to retire to the country. Before she finally moves, she wants to make sure of getting a decent sum from her successor for the fittings and furnishings. She's seen three possible tenants so far, but they're humming and hawing, and that gives you the chance of stepping in and snapping up the flat.'

'Here we go again!' George sighed. 'The old, old story. Ten thousand francs' key-money for a couple of deal cupboards and a moth-eaten strip of carpet . . . How much does the old girl want?'

'Ten thousand francs; you've said it. But she might agree to less if you win her sympathy, and one look from the young man beside you should go right to her heart.'

The pressure of Bobby's elbow grew stronger. George Thiriet was still thinking, balancing the pros and cons. The housing shortage had created these illegal demands, they had become the accepted thing, but he still rebelled against the idea of spending every penny he possessed simply to obtain the right to take over a lease. Even so, perhaps this chance encounter had brought the end of their long nightmare.

'It's a splendid flat,' the stranger insisted.

'Right,' said George. 'I'll pay, then if the lady agrees to move . . . but that leaves the vital question unanswered – will the Company agree to let me into the Belloy Private Estate as a bona fide tenant?'

'I'm an old friend of the manager,' the man answered with a slight smile. 'He's an obliging sort of a bloke who doesn't take advantage of his position. If he doesn't object the flat'll be yours in four or five days, or even sooner.'

'And how much will his commission cost me?' George asked sceptically.

'The gentleman concerned will think himself more than rewarded by the delight of your wife and family.'

George and his son still would not believe their good luck. It was no more than an idle pavement conversation with a kind-hearted stranger. The latter politely raised his black hat to expose his freshly trimmed prickles.

'I'm not Father Christmas!' he laughed. 'I'm just Henri

Dupont, South Paris Area-Manager of Metropolitan Properties.'

George apologized profusely. He was sorely tempted. Nonetheless he was rather bewildered by the suddenness of the offer and not even Bobby beside him could bring him to a snap decision.

'I'll have to talk it over with my wife first,' he said uncertainly.

'Would you like to see the flat now?' suggested the obliging Monsieur Dupont. 'Then you'll know what you're being offered. If you find the lady's demands not unreasonable, and if you for your part will do what she expects, the whole thing can be settled in twenty-four hours by no more than the exchange of signatures at the foot of a lease.'

'Come on, Daddy!' Bobby cried eagerly.

George looked at his watch.

'I can take you there in my car,' Monsieur Dupont suggested. 'It's only a few minutes away.'

He led them over to a black Peugeot parked on the other side of the square where it gleamed in the rosy glow from the hairdresser's. George got in the front seat next to the magician, Dupont. Bobby had the back to himself. The car turned the corner of the Boulevard Champaubert and slowly ascended the new thoroughfare, bordered by gardens and blocks of flats with their windows aglow, cutting through the mushroom town of Puisay like some triumphal way. Monsieur Dupont stopped only for a moment at the main Post Office to telephone his tenant.

'Madame Papadakis is at home,' he said when he came back. 'You'll see, she's a delightful lady and although she's inclined to snap at you she really has a heart of gold.'

'You're telling me!' exclaimed the outraged Bobby. 'Wanting ten thousand francs as a good-bye present; that's a bit much, if you ask me!'

The two grown-ups chuckled indulgently.

'I have to turn a blind eye to that sort of thing,' sighed Monsieur Dupont. 'As far as you, my dear sir, are concerned please don't let your surprise be too obvious, or you may make her change her mind very quickly.'

The Belloy Private Estate stood with its eight blocks of flats in a checker-board pattern, white battlements against the darker backcloth of the park. Monsieur Dupont steered his 404 into the car-park beside Block No. 6 and led the silent Thiriets inside. The reception hall on the ground-floor opened, through tall glass doors, on to a terrace and a garden enclosed by the block. The walls, encased in marble, gleamed in the gold of the concealed lighting. It's too grand for us, George thought with a shudder of alarm which even made him forget to keep an eye on his son. But the man from Metropolitan Properties had taken Bobby by the hand, and the youngster walked beside him into this fairy palace, his eyes widening in amazement.

One of the three lifts took them all up to the eighth floor. The widow Papadakis must have been lying in wait behind her door, for they had hardly rung before it was opened. She had so intimidating an air, with her aquiline features, black dress and raven-black hair, that George Thiriet felt himself quite paralysed by shyness. Bobby thought she was younger than Monsieur Dupont had made out. Behind her, he could see a series of brightly lit rooms in all the chaos of an impending move.

'My dear sir,' she said to George in a loud affected voice with a trace of a Russian accent, 'my dear sir, I have not had the honour of meeting you before, but you impress me most favourably and the lad with you is as neat and smart as a young prince. And of course since Monsieur Dupont answers for you it would be most ungracious of me to exclude you from the running . . . Come in!'

She took them on a conducted tour of the flat at lightning speed, flinging open the doors to rooms and cupboards, bumping into the furniture and deafening her visitors with a stream of chatter that re-echoed shrilly from rooms too large for her.

Bobby brought up the rear, his clear eye noting the size and shape of each room, the number of windows, the luxurious fittings of kitchen and bathroom and the forty-foot balcony outside. It only needed a 'yes' and a rapid agreement between the grown-ups for all this to belong to the cave-dwellers from the Rue Mirandole.

This was what Madame Papadakis was expecting and now she started to talk about her five hundred square feet of carpet and her oak panelled cupboards.

'Look what I have to leave behind. Brand new, as you can see, and I don't think I'm profiteering if I try to get back ten of the fifteen thousand francs they cost me.'

George Thiriet kept a cool head on his shoulders. He was so used to looking over houses and flats, all to no purpose, that he was not going to be caught napping.

'I'm quite ready to put down my money,' he said firmly, 'since it seems a fair bargain. But I want to make sure of one or two things before I do.'

'*I* don't want your money!' Madame Papadakis exclaimed in tones of injured dignity. 'I'm just asking you for a small sum to help with my removal expenses. There's a slight difference . . .'

'Not for me, there isn't,' George answered dryly. 'The money's coming from *my* wallet and it's the result of five years' hardship for all my family. I'm not risking losing it in something that's not quite above board.'

Madame Papadakis swelled with rage and her eyes flashed fire. Bobby hunched his shoulders in the background and waited for the explosion. Luckily Monsieur Dupont took care to smooth things down.

'You're quite right to be so cautious,' he told George. 'But there's no need to worry, nothing can be done without Metropolitan Properties' consent, that's to say my own, and you know you have it in full. This being the case, it's understood

between us that you pay no money until you have on the one hand a properly drawn-up lease and on the other, the keys of the flat. So it's really Madame Papadakis who has to trust your word until the deal is completed.'

George seemed convinced and his weary features relaxed.

'When? he asked, with deep feeling. Too often he had seen his dream flat slip through his fingers because he had been too slow in making up his mind.

Madama Papadakis agreed to make arrangements at once, and they heard her discussing dates on the telephone with a removal firm.

'They say they can do it tomorrow,' she said at last as she

turned to face them. 'Otherwise it will have to be the end of next week. It's up to you.'

By now Bobby was only listening with half an ear. He was staring in surprise at a big black cat curled up on the top of a cabinet in a dark corner of the sitting-room. In a few seconds the picture altered as the black cat opened a pair of yellow eyes to gaze at the boy with a complete lack of interest.

Bobby knew that such fastidious animals need always to be approached with the greatest care. He tried a gentle chirrup. The black cat sat and blinked. Bobby grew bolder, scratched him behind the ears and told him what a beautiful fellow he was. No claw darted out, and his stroking released a powerful purr which betrayed the cat's friendly disposition.

The voices in the hall resounded in happy mutual congratulation.

'The flat will be cleared completely by tomorrow afternoon,' Madame Papadakis was saying. 'So we can meet again tomorrow to settle things finally. Here, if you like, at the same time.'

'Right!' Monsieur Dupont agreed. 'I'll bring the papers and all we need do is sign on the dotted line.'

'I'll have the money,' George Thiriet promised. 'So it's all fixed for tomorrow evening.'

He turned to call Bobby.

'Where have you been?'

'In the sitting-room. I was making friends with the cat.'

Madame Papadakis looked bewildered.

'A cat?' she said. 'The child must be imagining things. There's never been a cat in this flat. Anyway I can't stand animals . . .'

They went to look, but the ghost cat had vanished.

'B . . . but he was there,' Bobby stuttered. He was puzzled. 'A lovely black cat with yellow eyes. He was purring so loud I'm sure you could have heard him in the hall.'

'It must have been a neighbour's cat,' suggested Monsieur Dupont. 'The brute jumped from their balcony to yours and slipped inside.'

They said good-bye to the widow. George was in a great hurry to tell the good news to his wife and the three older children. His skinny figure was radiant with happiness.

'Well, this time you're out of the wood,' Monsieur Dupont told him as he led them towards the 404. 'The Belloy Private Estate awaits you and you can count yourselves as good as there already. Remember where we're meeting tomorrow – Block 6, eighth floor, flat 121' – and he flung wide his arms – 'Your flat!'

'Good-bye Rue Mirandole!' Bobby carolled and danced for joy.

2

The keys of Paradise

JACQUES and Laurent came out of school that night and made their melancholy way towards the Rue Mirandole. As usual they took the long way round the Avenue de Paris to enjoy the bright lights outside until the very last moment. The cramped conditions in which the family lived, crowded into poky, gloomy quarters, had drained them of their natural cheerfulness. Even when they came home with Bobby their chatter stilled once the grimy doorway of Number 33 hove in sight.

'It makes me sick,' Jacques was saying, as they turned the corner of the Rue du Général Tuboeuf. 'It's the third time the Barons have asked us out and I don't know how we can return their hospitality. I know they don't expect a palace, but our hovel is the limit. We'd have to ask the others to go out if we were to sit Charlie and Lily down to a decent meal.'

Jacques Thiriet was tall for seventeen, very fair and well built, and his parents sometimes wondered how so sturdy a specimen could have grown undamaged in the gloomy basement in which they had mouldered for the last five years. His younger brother looked almost weedy beside him. His smooth black hair set off his pale face. Nonetheless, Laurent's slim figure housed a livelier, more forceful character. As a small boy he had been the terror of the Rue Mirandole, and now, at fifteen, he was finding school discipline a burden.

'The Barons are in no hurry to take pot-luck with the Thiriet family,' he laughed. 'They can wait another month at least. Daddy'll invite them to our house-warming in one of the skyscrapers on the Place Brémonteir, that's all!'

Jacques shrugged.

'Still think he'll find a flat? Short of the walls of No. 33 collapsing about the landlord's ears, we'll be stuck in the Rue Mirandole for ever.'

'Daddy's tried so hard,' Laurent answered, 'that he must get something really good or really bad and what could be worse . . .'

The hall-way of No. 33 Rue Mirandole was like a dug-out. A solitary bulb cast a yellowish light that hardly pierced the gloom of the long corridor which led to the series of tiny ground-floor flats. The Thiriets' was at the very end. Sophie and her daughter Isabelle had just got home from the office in the Avenue de Paris where they both worked. As soon as she heard the dragging footsteps of the boys she opened the door and the living-room was as crowded as a railway carriage. Her sons kissed their mother and told her about their day.

'We'll wait supper for your father and Bobby,' said Madame Thiriet.

'They'd better not be long, I'm hungry as a horse,' Belle announced.

She was even fairer than Jacques, inheriting her mother's trim figure and an ability to laugh at everything, which she shared with the baby of the family, Bobby. Now she earned her living, the boys did not dare tease their elder sister. Belle was old enough to have left home, but family ties were too strong – despite the cramped quarters in which life depended on mutual concessions to be bearable.

The living-room was twelve foot by nine. During the daytime, the parents' bed folded back against the left-hand wall and this did allow some movement, albeit restricted to the very minimum. On the right-hand wall stood the principal piece of furniture, a monumental mass of worm-eaten wood, a Breton dresser bequeathed by a distant relative with a doubtful sense of humour. Then came the gas fire in an imitation marble fireplace and six chairs stacked one on top of the other to the ceiling. At the far end, on either side of the fanlight window, which even at midday was niggardly with its day-light, hard-board partitions concealed one corner for the cooking stove and the other for the wash-basin common to them all. Next door was the children's room. This was no more than a six-foot wide passage divided by white plastic curtains.

In front, under the skylight, were Jacques' and Laurent's bunks and beside them the camp bed which Bobby was now beginning to find too short for his long coltish legs. At the end was Belle's narrow divan, a hanging cupboard and a shelf for her most treasured possessions.

To make up for the lack of space all was immaculately tidy, and spotless cleanliness transformed the slum conditions in which they lived.

'The place seems to shrink around us every day,' was George Thiriet's favourite joke. 'In another couple of years, the children will have grown so big they'll burst the house at the seams. It's time we moved.'

They were all of the same opinion, but ill-luck so closely dogged the footsteps of the head of the family that not a flicker of hope awoke in them on the evenings when he came in to announce,

'It looks as though we'll be moving soon . . .'

While Belle and her mother chattered as they prepared the evening meal, Jacques and Laurent worked for a while in their corridor room. But soon hunger drove the two boys out of their retreat.

'Aren't we ever going to eat? It's after eight o'clock . . . What on earth are Daddy and Bobby up to?'

'Fred must have given them a perm,' Belle laughed.

'If they aren't back in five minutes we'll lay the table, for a start,' said Sophie Thiriet.

This five minutes' grace had more than elapsed when Belle

and her brothers began to erect a complicated piece of equipment on which the ingenuity of the head of the house had been lavished. The Thiriets' dining table had only two legs – folding ones of course! When not in use it was secured by a pair of strong hooks flush against the door leading to the passage. At meal times the erection team would set it level on its two feet, the free end engaged in stout slots nailed to the door. Only when the whole contraption had been strengthened and supported and all the flaps locked and bolted into position could the cloth be put on and the six places laid.

If anyone came in late, this did not mean clearing and dismantling the table, for the door opened outwards. So, on the word of command, everyone got up and held the table, the crockery and the cutlery steady. The end was disengaged from the slot as the door was eased open. The latecomer crept in on all-fours between the others and surfaced at his place. Practice had so perfected the whole operation that the cave-dwellers of the Rue Mirandole looked upon it as a great joke.

'No nonsense, now,' Belle told her brother. 'Don't forget to lock the door properly . . .'

'Come and get it!' Sophie Thiriet called as she carried in a steaming tureen.

Jacques carefully unstacked the chairs, passed three over to his brother, and set the others on his side of the table. Then they all sat down, sniffing the savour of the soup – beef and carrots – that had been simmering on the stove behind the partition. But nobody heard a front door shut close by, round the corner of the Rue Mirandole.

George Thiriet and his young son had come in quietly hugging the walls. They were both picturing to themselves the rapture of the rest of the family and the hugs and kisses that would stifle the heroes of the evening.

'Stay behind me,' George told Bobby. 'Don't say a word,

and try not to grin. I'm going to knock them cold with the good news.'

He reached the end of the corridor and swung the door wide open. His abrupt movement set off a crash like thunder in the 'rat-hole'. Jacques and Laurent saw the table leap up from under their noses as they fell backwards with shouts of alarm. The soup tureen bounced up to the skylight as crockery and cutlery cascaded on to the floor with a violent crash and clatter. Sophie Thiriet managed to step clear in time to catch the flying carafe of wine. Belle alone sat at a non-existent table, clutching her spoon in open-mouthed alarm.

'You call that locking the door properly!' she yelled at last, and glared at her brothers.

'But I did give the key a turn,' Jacques protested.

'You didn't turn it far enough! The door opened and shot our supper on to the ceiling.'

'Well, it wouldn't have happened if the lock had been properly oiled.'

'Daddy, you broke the rule,' Laurent said accusingly. 'If anyone comes in after eight o'clock they've got to knock three times to let us know they're there.'

They turned on George Thiriet, who stood still and sheepish in the doorway. Behind thick lenses his short-sighted eyes blinked owlishly.

'I . . . I . . . I've f . . . found a flat,' he stuttered in self-defence. 'We . . . we'll be m . . . moving the day after to-morrow.'

His news fell completely flat. It must have been at least the hundredth time that he had come home with as definite a promise. The others could not hold back their howl of laughter, and the tragedy of the retractable table was soon forgotten. Then Bobby came into the lamp-light, his grin splitting a face that seemed rounder now that he had had his hair cut.

'Daddy really has found one,' he said calmly. 'A smashing

flat! We've been round and measured up every room. It's ours. It'll all be fixed up tomorrow night.'

It was the turn of the others to look sheepish. Then they closed in on George and Bobby, firing incoherent questions at them. The Belloy Private Estate? They wouldn't believe it. You could put the whole of the Rue Mirandole 'rat-hole' into the kitchen? Incredible. Hot water by the gallon? Carpet that was nearly brand new and cupboards with self-closing doors?

'That's unnecessarily luxurious,' Sophie said.

'But we've got to take it,' sighed the embarrassed George. 'Yes, that confounded carpet's going to make a hole in my bank balance, but we've got to take it – and the rest of the fittings. We only got preferential treatment from the present tenant of the flat on condition we did – and of course from the Manager, too!'

The lingering doubts vanished when he showed them Monsieur Dupont's card. Then the whole family surrendered to their rapture. The collapsible table was set back on its two legs, and they ended up by having a hilarious meal from what was left of the crockery. Midnight found them still sitting up round a large sheet of white paper covered in pencilled scribble. George Thiriet had laid down a large plan of the flat from the measurements taken on the spot four hours before. One by one with sparkling eyes, each was assigned his future domain.

'Belle shall have the room at the end that overlooks the private garden. The biggest, at the front, will be for the boys, so they'll have a fitted washbasin to themselves. We shall use the room in the middle, the present drawing-room, as our living-cum-dining-room. Your parents are going to have the room at the other end, it's next to the bathroom. I haven't forgotten the balcony.' George giggled like a small boy. 'We can put a garden table out there and have our dinner outside in the cool of the evening all through the summer. There's going to be a big difference from this black hole in the Rue Mirandole!'

'What about furniture?' asked his wife.

'We'll have to make do with what we've got for a start. Then we'll furnish our new home as fast as we can save the

money – a bed first, and then a sofa, some armchairs, a desk for the boy, a wardrobe for Belle.'

His audience listened intently. The flat they had coveted so long was shadowy no more, but there in all its fascinating detail. Each was already filling this in as his or her fancy and notions of comfort dictated, and ecstatically imagining how they would shed the gloomy past as they rose into the eighth heaven of the Belloy Private Estate. Sophie cut short their dreams as she pointed to Bobby, fast asleep in his chair, his head lolling on his right shoulder.

They all felt the next day fall into the pattern of those busy exciting occasions like the eve of Christmas or Easter, or going away for the summer holidays. Wisely the three day-boys at the Lycée Alfred-Jarry were kept well away from the centre of operations, but each in his own way felt the magic intoxication which made the minutes now flash past, now drag agonizingly. Bobby went to the bottom of the history class for shamelessly marrying Anne of Austria to Louis XVI. Laurent was caught red-handed in the act of pinning a paper tail to a class-monitor's coat. He merely smiled when he was given two hours' detention. Only Jacques kept a reasonably cool head.

The three brothers had sworn not to say a word to the others until the red-letter day on which they were to move in. The eldest, however, ignored this at the behest of social duty and carefully wrote out an announcement which was passed right round the form until it reached its destination, Charlie Baron, Managing Editor of the *P.S.N.*

Jacques, Laurent and Robert Thiriet
are happy to announce a change of address to
Flat 121, No. 6 Belloy Private Estate

Charlie put the paper in his brief-case and sent his answer back to Jacques by the same route.

Too late. Tomorrow's issue has gone to press. Your announcement will appear in next week's gossip column. My! Old Man Thiriet must have come into a nice lot of money to jump from the Rue Mirandole to the Belloy Private Estate! Good work! We'll be near neighbours so I'll want you on Tuesday evenings to prepare the P.S.N. *for press.*

His classmates showed the same kindly amazement, tinged in some cases with mild disbelief. This was what finally soured Jacques' pleasure and pricked the bubble of his high spirits. He imagined the worst happening – one more disappointment to add to all the rest – the widow Papadakis heartlessly changing her mind – the incorruptible Area-Manager of Metropolitan Properties demanding a last-minute 'sweetener' of astronomical size, and so forth and so on. In short, he convinced himself that they would be thrust back into the misery of their basement for another five or six years of sunless days and airless nights.

Laurent was bewildered by his gloomy expression when they met after school.

'Whatever's the matter with you?'

'With me? Nothing! I'm only thinking Father's sure to have mucked things up again. His four-room luxury flat'll slip through our fingers, you see. Do you really think we're smart enough yet for the Belloy Private Estate?'

So Jacques argued his case, basing it upon all their previous disappointments. Laurent was not easily discouraged, but this pessimism was infectious and his face lengthened gloomily. They both made off for the gate on the Rue Pochet to snatch Bobby out of the eddy of his classmates. The baby of the family had all the complete confidence of his age, and he laughed when he heard the others croaking like a pair of birds of ill-omen.

'You're cracked, you two. This time Daddy really has made up his mind to go all out. He knows he'll never get another chance like this one and neither the old girl nor the manager are going to stop him.'

The trio made straight for the dug-out in the Rue Mirandole. Belle was already there, smiling as she filled a battered old trunk with her dresses.

'Mummy and Daddy took a half-day off to get things straight,' she told the boys. 'They'd so much to do – draw the money out of the bank – get a removal man for tomorrow morning, and that wasn't easy – let the landlord of Number 33 know . . .'

Bobby burst out laughing.

'I'd like to see how that old skinflint took it. He's made us pay the earth for his cellars.'

'Anyway, it all went off all right. If you'd been in five minutes earlier you'd have seen Mummy and Daddy. Monsieur Dupont came round in his 404 to take them straight up to Belloy. Apparently Madame Papadakis' removal men have worked like blacks and there's an empty flat waiting for the Thiriet family. Now, just follow my example.'

'Starting to pack already?' Jacques asked delightedly. 'It just doesn't seem possible!'

'That's Daddy's instructions. At nine o'clock tomorrow he wants us to be out of here in one fell swoop.'

Jacques was tall enough to pull down the suitcases stacked on top of the Breton dresser. Methodically they emptied drawers, cupboards and boxes, took down the curtains, ornaments and pictures, dismantled clothes-racks, mangle and shelves in a gale of laughter and cheers and with as much giddy haste as if the removal van had already been ticking over outside Number 33 Rue Mirandole.

An hour passed.

'If you ask me, Daddy's taking a long time to sign two scraps of paper and count ten thousand francs into the widow's skinny claw,' Jacques suddenly exclaimed as he burrowed into the shelves of the dresser. No longer was there the slightest trace of anxiety in his remark, merely a slight iritation at the long, nerve-straining delay.

'Maybe Madame Papadakis sealed the bargain with a ceremonial glass of port,' hissed Bobby.

Ten more minutes passed. Nobody heard the two twilight messengers arrive and make their stealthy way along the dimly lit passage of the tenement like a couple of thieves. The door opened soundlessly and a blast of cold night air swept in. Belle and her brothers were crouching over the last suitcase. They jerked upright, their eyes staring in alarm. George and Sophie Thiriet stood still and silent in the doorway. The only sign on their faces was the breathlessness of their hurried return, but their hearts were full. Then George slowly put out his right hand which had been hidden behind his back, and offered the children two bunches of shining keys that clinked as he held them up.

'I've done it!' His voice was husky. 'The flat's ours. You've really deserved it.'

The cheers of his offspring set the whole neighbourhood stirring and he quickly had to shut the family into its rat-hole. Hugged and questioned until they were giddy, George and his wife had to sit down a moment to recover from the excitement of the day.

'It all went like clockwork. Dear old Madame Papadakis was the anxious one, I'm sure. She paced up and down her empty flat until she had the money for her carpet safe.'

'She had the nerve to take all that money of yours!' an indignant Bobby exclaimed.

'And how!' His father laughed. 'She was on to my bundles of banknotes like a hawk. She counted the money over and over again, but she wouldn't take a fraction off her price. But we've been through all that: now let's forget it.'

'What about the manager?'

'Monsieur Dupont is a real brick. He kept his word. He'd got two copies of the lease with him. I initialled and signed them both. He'll be sending me my copy when it's been properly registered. So you see that side of things is all in order.'

'When I think of all the trouble that man went to for us!' Sophie said.

'I can honestly say he guided me round all the pitfalls in that complicated business,' George admitted. 'He was even so kind as to give us a lift there and back in his car to save time. Your mother and I were quite amazed. It's something we shan't forget in a hurry, not nowadays when public benefactors are a dying race. Once we're in the flat we'll have to show Monsieur Dupont that we haven't forgotten all he's done for us . . . We'll invite him to our house-warming.'

Then he congratulated Belle and her brothers on having packed up so well.

'Arranging the move was the most trying part of all,' he said. 'I spent half the afternoon dashing round before I could get hold of a little man from Bagneux who promised to let me have his lorry for tomorrow morning. There'll only be the driver and his mate so we'll all have to give a hand.'

'What about the Shylock of Number 33?' Laurent asked, poking a mocking finger at the ceiling.

'Your mother went upstairs two or three times to tell him the news, but he was out. For form's sake I'll write him a farewell letter and one of you can send it to him by registered post.'

'Ask him for something for the furniture and fittings!' Bobby's suggestion made them all laugh.

'Why?' said honest George. 'All we're leaving is this worm-eaten old dresser and it'll fall to pieces as soon as anyone touches it. Anyway, between ourselves, it'd rather upset me to squeeze anything out of whoever's unlucky enough to take our place in the "rat-hole".'

Belle looked at her watch. Eight o'clock already and the boys were dribbling with hunger.

'Shall we have dinner right away?'

'Let's finish clearing the monument first,' Jacques suggested. 'It won't take ten minutes.'

There was a light-hearted whirl of activity round the dresser. George and Sophie finished packing their own cases, while the children piled the household linen into a wicker basket. When all was strapped down, the master of the house inspected the interior of the ancient piece of furniture for the last time. Then he solemnly closed the two badly-fitting doors which creaked above the hubbub of the room. As he turned he was surprised to see how sad his wife looked.

'Don't let's leave the poor old dresser behind,' she murmured. 'It wouldn't be nice, you know how much I like it.'

Tears glittered in her eyes. George tried to reason with her.

'Your dresser will only take up space. The flat's bursting with cupboards. Belle and the boys won't want it in either of their rooms.'

But Sophie dug her toes in. She had childhood memories which made her fond of the family heirloom.

'We could put the dresser in the hall. It won't get in anybody's way. On the left-hand side there's a recess about six feet wide between the living-room and Belle's room.'

George frowned and looked at the plan he had drawn the evening before. The recess was not marked on it.

'From what I can remember, I don't think your dresser's going to fit,' he said.

'I'm sure it will!' claimed Sophie.

'It's quite easy to make certain,' said Laurent, who was burning to see the flat, 'Let's go over and measure it up.'

'If your recess is the right size,' added Jacques, 'we can move the dresser with the rest of the stuff, and Mummy won't have any regrets about leaving.'

'Good idea,' George agreed. Turning his back on the older children he stared at the conscientious Bobby.

'You know how to get there.' He winked. 'Here are the

keys and a tape measure! Catch the 188 and get off at the end of the Boulevard Champaubert. It won't take you five minutes. Measure the hall, and don't go to sleep on Madame Papadakis' carpet. In the meantime we'll finish packing.'

3
Flat 121

THE route was firmly fixed in Bobby's mind, and the closer he got to the Belloy Private Estate the more his heart swelled with joy. At the far end of the boulevard the eight tall blocks stood like some golden gate, their twelve storeys studded with lighted windows, with the dark mass of the park behind them to emphasize their height and the snowy whiteness of their façades.

The entrance hall of No. 6 was alive with movement. Well-dressed, smiling people, who had nothing in common with the cave-dwellers of the Rue Mirandole, greeted one another as they passed. But Bobby did not feel shy for a moment; he had only to touch the keys in his pocket to have all the confidence in the world.

The same lift in which he had travelled the night before took him up to the eighth floor. With him was a fat gentleman who was going higher and they parted with a cheerful good night. Bobby whistled as he hurried down the brightly lit corridor which served the left wing of the building. It was empty. Flat 121 was at the very end. Through neighbouring doors, people's voices filtered, mingling with snatches of music or the monotone of a TV announcer.

With great care he produced his bunch of keys. The biggest slid into the mortice lock but refused to turn in either direction. Very surprised, Bobby tried the flat little key in the spring-lock, but it only went in half-an-inch or so and then stuck. 'I must have got the wrong floor,' Bobby said to himself and glanced round.

Then his eye fell on the small brass plate discreetly screwed to the door-frame below the bell-push. *Monsieur and Madame Papadakis*. He smiled. The old girl must have overlooked it or simply left it behind in the rush of moving. Reassured, Bobby once more inserted the big key and juggled with it in an attempt to unlock the mortice – still without success.

Suddenly a metallic click jerked him backwards. Someone was inside the flat and turning the spring-lock. The door half opened on to a well-lit hall. It was not Madame Papadakis who stood in the doorway, but a white-haired lady with a look of astonishment on her gentle face. At once she noticed the bunch of keys Bobby held in his right hand.

'You've got the wrong floor, dear,' she said smiling. 'Or perhaps the wrong block.'

'I d . . . don't think so,' Bobby stuttered. 'Madame Papadakis moved out this afternoon and Metropolitan Properties leased her flat to my father, Monsieur Thiriet. We're moving in tomorrow morning.'

The old lady began to laugh and pulled the door wide open.

'Come, come, a joke's a joke,' she said, her cheeks going quite pink. '*I* am Madame Papadakis.'

Behind her, Bobby was amazed to see the flat which he had visited the night before with his father and Monsieur Dupont. There was the fine furniture gleaming, the carpets, the knick-knacks and the Persian rugs.

The black cat had come back too. Snugly curled up in an armchair he watched Bobby, blinking his yellow eyes with a faraway look, neither mocking nor angry, the essence of mystery.

At last another figure came into the light – a grey-haired gentleman wearing a smoking jacket. His face was swarthy, and his jet black eyes sparkled under their tufted white brows.

'Would you like to tell my husband your story?' said the old lady.

Bobby made a clumsy bow to the newcomer but his greeting was hardly tactful.

'I thought you'd been dead and buried six months ago!'

His bewilderment spread to the Papadakis. The husband drew himself up.

'What! What! I'd just like to know who's been telling you these fairy stories . . .'

'It was Madame Papadakis – the other one. The one who asked us to look over the flat yesterday and was supposed to move out this afternoon.'

'Well, you can see nobody's moved out.'

'But an hour ago when Daddy came to sign the lease for the manager and pay the lady for the furniture and fittings the flat was quite empty. Anyway it's been properly leased to us by Metropolitan Properties.'

'This flat leased!' the gentleman exclaimed angrily. 'There's as little question of that as there is of our moving out, and for one very good reason – I've bought the freehold. Now stop worrying us. Play your practical jokes on the neighbours, if you want to.'

'I'm not playing any jokes,' pleaded Bobby, now close to tears.

His distress touched Monsieur Papadakis.

'Perhaps you're not, but someone neither of us knows has played a nasty trick on all of us. My wife and I have just come back from a visit. Unknown to us, somebody has used our name and our flat to deceive your father disgracefully . . . Come inside a minute, please. We must try to sort this out. To start with, where do you live?'

Bobby obeyed, not knowing what else to do, and gave them the address in the Rue Mirandole. From the hall he heard the old man telephoning the police station, and the sinister word 'Confidence trick' entered the conversation several times. As the dream of tomorrow's happiness melted, Bobby's head drooped and he began to cry soundlessly.

The real Madame Papadakis led him to an armchair and tried hard to comfort him. Then the black cat jumped up on his knees, and snuggled down, purring delightedly. Bobby stroked him, letting his tears fall unchecked on the gleaming black fur.

A quarter of an hour later his whole family swept down the corridor behind a burly little man, obviously a plain-clothes policeman from his cynical expression. Poor George and his wife were completely downcast, while Belle and her brothers shook with rage.

'This is the flat I visited, right enough,' George thundered, 'and leased and paid for – and at a price, too! It was quite empty an hour ago. The manager himself gave me the keys and I locked it behind me, myself, when I left.'

'Try them, then.' The policeman was all amusement. 'We'll soon see if it's the right door.'

George tried his pair, but they worked no better than Bobby's. His face went white.

'It's witchcraft! It's the same flat. I'm sure of it. The only difference is that it's filled up again like a jack-in-the-box with the very same furniture I saw on my first visit last night. Hang on! I'm not imagining things – there's the name on the door-frame – Papadakis. It was there when I left an hour ago!'

'It's an easy matter to unscrew a name plate and screw it back again,' said the policeman nonchalantly.

Meanwhile the caretaker for Block 6 had arrived on the scene with a second plain-clothes man. He himself had the face and figure of a retired policeman. He greeted the Papadakis politely, confirmed their identity, certified that they did in fact own the flat and furthermore that they had been away and only returned that very morning. This removed any suspicion of their complicity in the by-play of the night before.

'It still doesn't prove it,' George protested despairingly. 'They've got their flat back, but I don't know where my ten thousand francs have gone.'

'But you should have talked to the caretaker first of all,' the policeman answered. 'All this wouldn't have happened if . . .'

'Why should I have been suspicious? I'd got the manager on my side.'

'What manager?'

'Metropolitan Properties' manager,' George answered, playing his last card. 'Monsieur Dupont!'

'Never heard of him!' growled the caretaker. 'Anyway all the flats on the Estate are individually owned. The Property Company hasn't even got an office . . . You've been properly had!'

'And what about the empty flat we just visited?' Sophie Thiriet cut in.

'Yes,' the caretaker frowned, 'there is an empty flat in Block 6. It's right under this one.'

'Let's have a look at it then,' said the policeman.

The whole group went down to the floor below. Neighbours were beginning to be disturbed by all the tramping to and fro, and angry or curious faces appeared at half-open doors.

At the end of the corridor was a door identical with that of the Papadakis. Their name-plate was no longer there, but four fresh holes in the dark woodwork showed where it had been.

Once more George tried his keys. The door opened with the greatest of ease. There were the bare, light brown walls and the dark brown carpet with its fine, almost brand new sheen.

'Here we are!' the Thiriets cried out. 'This is the place.'

The caretaker stifled their hopes at once.

'This flat has just been bought from its original owners by a family from overseas. They should be moving in in a fortnight.'

'But we've leased it!' George bellowed, 'I signed the lease and paid the old hag who called herself Madame Papadakis for the fittings and furniture.'

'All right!' said one of the policemen. 'But you were let in with a bunch of false keys by a clever con-man who tricked you into thinking the seventh floor was the eighth. And that makes all the difference.'

'Better see the chief,' said the other. 'Yes, that means all of you, kids included.'

The humdrum run of day-to-day activities had not yet damped Monsieur Sinet's zeal.

He was still eager to play the master detective in his brand-new police station at Puisay. A bundle of carrots pilfered from the street market set him as purposefully on the warpath as a bank raid.

He could not hide his satisfaction at the sight of this mass delegation, but his face darkened as soon as he noticed an eleven-year-old ragamuffin hemmed in by two scowling elder brothers. All the misfortunes that had chequered his career as a police officer had been caused by birds of that feather.

The original telephone call from the Papadakis and a later one from his own officers had been enough to make quite clear to him the nature and method of the confidence trick. He began by taking George Thiriet to task. George looked a wretched figure, surrounded by his discomfited family.

'Don't you complain about losing your money! In a business like this, you're as much to blame as the man who tricked you. Your own honesty blinded you far more than the counterfeit kindness of the unknown crook who's made you the laughing stock of the Rue Mirandole. My dear sir, nowadays managers of property companies don't go round offering luxury flats to the first poor fool they meet. It's quite unthinkable! . . . Now describe the fellow.'

George and his wife somewhat bitterly gave a verbal picture of the kind-hearted gentleman who had so neatly fooled them, with his borrowed name, into mistaking one floor for another. The flat on the eighth floor had been the bait, the one below, so magically empty, had dispelled the last suspicions of the good old idiot who had paid out ten thousand francs in hard cash for five minutes of delightful dreams.

The Commissioner's questioning glance fell upon the Papadakis.

'We don't know him,' they replied stolidly.

Sinet turned to the homeless family.

'Did anyone else see him?'

'My youngest,' said George, and pointed to Bobby.

Sinet stared at the boy with deep distrust.

'Aha?' he said sarcastically. 'Now this fake manager who sells his fake keys so dearly, what did he look like?'

'He looked like a white hedgehog,' Bobby declared, wide-eyed and solemn.

Commissioner Sinet nearly fell off his chair. So this was it. In a flash he could see himself back in those dreadful days of the horse without a head.*

'A white hedgehog? Really, now?' He swallowed hastily. 'You don't see an animal like that every day of the week.'

'It's just my way of putting it,' Bobby explained. 'Actually, our public benefactor had a nice round pink face, spiky fair hair and two black button eyes so close together that they were rather like an animal's. So I find it easier to call him the White Hedgehog. But he may not have looked like that to you.'

Angry yet intrigued, Sinet frowned at him.

'Where should I have seen him?'

'In Fred's, the hairdresser's, last night. He was sitting right behind us having his prickles trimmed. You had a good fifteen minutes' view of the back of his head and side of his face in the mirror in front of you!'

To Bobby's amazement the policeman seemed only now to realize that this was the father and son he had run into so briefly in Monsieur Fred's hairdressing saloon.

'I remember, now I come to think of it.' He forced a laugh. 'You were sitting next to me pretending to read some rag called the *P.S.N.*'

And then, as though brushing off some fly, he returned to cross-question the chief witness as harshly as ever.

'Now tell me about the woman who invited you up to the flat on the eighth floor last night.'

George's description at once enlightened the real Papadakis.

'It's the Grand Duchess!' they exclaimed indignantly. 'Natasha Popv! Why, she was our housekeeper, always such

* See Paul Berna's book, *A hundred million francs.*

a nuisance. We sacked her six months ago for dishonesty. She must have taken an impression of our keys before she left. Oh, they know all about Natasha in the neighbourhood!'

'Then we may be able to pick her up pretty quickly,' Sinet said as he jotted down the information.

'What about the fake manager?' George asked.

'We'll trail his accomplice; she'll put us on his track sooner or later and then we'll pick them both up in one swoop. Now about your ten thousand francs, well I'm not going to raise any false hopes. With professional con-men it's lightly come, lightly go, and you can be pretty sure most of your money's gone already.'

George and his wife bowed their heads. This matter-of-fact statement set the seal on the catastrophe. Belle dabbed at reddened eyes. Jacques and Laurent clenched their fists, their youthful faces hardening in black rage.

'Was there anyone else with these two crooks when you first met them yesterday?' Sinet continued.

'Not a soul,' George answered, somewhat surprised.

'But there was,' Bobby suddenly broke in. 'There was the cat.'

Once more an angry Sinet turned in his chair.

'All we need in this deplorable business is an animal! What was the creature like? Did he make a statement to you?'

'No, but he seemed quite at home in the flat.'

Bobby possessed a sharp eye for detail and his remark intrigued the Commissioner.

'What did he look like?'

'A big black cat with yellow eyes. I wasn't a bit surprised to see him again a little while ago in the same flat.'

'He's right,' the two policemen agreed. 'We noticed him as well when we got there. He was asleep in the boy's lap.'

'Do you own this cat?' Sinet asked the Papadakis.

'Of course we do! That's Toddles. We've had him since our Siamese died of old age. Toddles never leaves us and goes visiting with us in his basket. My husband and I adore cats.'

This was beyond Sinet.

'When did you get back?'

'This morning, with our Toddles in his basket.'

'Then someone's lying,' the Commissioner growled, and glared at Bobby. 'Are you saying that that cat was in the upper flat last night?'

'I'm not lying,' Bobby protested. 'I did see the cat there, and I stroked it.'

'And the one tonight?'

'He jumped up into my lap like an old pal. I thought he recognized me.'

'We took Toddles away with us.' Madame Papadakis was positive. 'The cat the little boy's talking about must have been a stray. Perhaps Madame Breton, the caretaker's wife, shut it in by mistake when she aired the flat. Anyway, it wasn't there when we came back with Toddles.'

Bobby seemed upset.

'At first s . . . sight,' he stammered, 'I c . . . couldn't see any difference.'

'Of course there was,' Madame Papadakis patiently insisted. 'It wasn't the same cat just now; that was our Toddles.'

'Anyway,' one of the policemen broke in with a laugh, 'there's nothing so like one black cat as another black cat.'

Sinet silenced him with a look.

'Let's keep to the point. When all's said and done it wasn't the cat that got its claws into the ten thousand francs, so there's no need for me to mention the animal in the official report of the case. At the moment the main thing is to lay hands on the two thieves as soon as we can. They're no novices and if Records have their photographs, fingerprints and descriptions on file, we should get them sooner or later . . . Now you can go.'

His bad temper found its outlet in his unjustifiable irritation, in the first place with George Thiriet for having allowed himself to be robbed so stupidly, with the Papadakis for being in the clear, with the caretaker for only having one pair of eyes and legs to take care of the twelve storeys of Block 6, and with the stupid cat that had appeared from nowhere. But his most bitter resentment was reserved for the two crooks – on whom he would doubtless never set eyes again – for having pulled off their crime in Puisay, just to make things difficult for him – Commissioner Sinet himself!

'We're really terribly sorry for what's happened,' Monsieur Papadakis was saying as they stood outside the police-station. 'If there's anything I can do . . .'

'You could always refund the ten thousand francs I've just lost,' George retorted bitterly. 'But that's asking too much I imagine.'

They parted on this note, the Papadakis and the caretaker returning to the Belloy Private Estate, the Thiriet family wending their melancholy way to the Rue Mirandole.

Once there, the sight of their possessions all packed up brought tears to their eyes. Now they had to unpack and carefully replace them all, a task which took twice as long as the previous packing. It was not until midnight that the 'rat-hole' resumed its usual appearance and that they realized they had not had time for a bite to eat in all the upheaval.

'What a way to see the new day in,' grumbled Laurent as he lowered the collapsible table.

George hung his head, ashamed at the reproaches that remained unspoken on the others' lips.

'One good thing – the landlord didn't get our notice,' Belle remarked. 'We should have been in a fix!'

All six sat down at the table. They had no appetite for their food; they hardly said a word, and then only whispered; it was like a funeral supper. There was a long silence, the herald of an outburst of despair.

'Well, I think we're jolly comfortable here in the Rue Mirandole!' piped Bobby.

There was a burst of laughter. The supper party suddenly felt their spirits rise and they all tried to console George Thiriet.

'There you are,' Sophie said kindly. 'Nobody blames you. You were tricked, but you were only trying to do the best for us. That nasty-looking commissioner would have been caught quicker than you.'

George took all the blame.

'Whatever you say, I'm a prize idiot and you're the ones to suffer for my simplicity. As you know, those ten thousand francs were our entire savings. Now that they've gone up in smoke, we're as poor as we were when we first moved in. That was five years ago and it was only meant to be temporary, but some spite seems intent on keeping us here . . . All I can say is I hope we can steer clear of illness.'

Belle and her young brothers were hit hard. Their father had exactly summed up their predicament. To an ordinary, hard-working family, in which there had never been money to burn, such a sudden loss could well bring appalling consequences. The boys soon got over the first shock in a healthy outbursts of anger. Jacques clenched his teeth and stared his younger brothers in the eye.

'Whatever happens we'll catch those two jokers,' he told them, 'and we're going to make them pay dearly for our returned trip to the Rue Mirandole.'

'The world's a big place,' Belle sighed.

'It's often too small for crooks who think they can get away with anything. Why, our public benefactor and that hag could be only a hundred yards away at this very moment, in a comfortable studio flat in the Boulevard Champaubert splitting Father's cash between them.'

'After a day like this,' Laurent said coldly, 'they're probably sitting back with their feet up.'

'We'll get them!' Jacques repeated.

'I'm raring to go,' Bobby announced, smacking his chest. 'Just let them show their faces . . .'

Jacques and Laurent shrugged pityingly.

'Suppose you bumped into your old friend the White Hedgehog round the corner of the Rue Pochet . . . What'd you do?'

'First of all I'd say a polite "hullo" . . .'

'And then?'

'The Hedgehog'd dart off. Then, woof, I'd trip him up. He'd go smack on the pavement. I'd jump on top of him with twenty of the others and we'd give it to him good and proper. Don't you worry! The fire brigade would get there quicker than Commissioner Sinet!'

4
P.S.N.

NEXT day, instead of weeping on their classmates' shoulders, the three Thiriets determined to keep a scrupulous silence about the events of the night before. As they came out of school that evening Jacques bore his brothers off to a new block on the Boulevard Champaubert where the Barons, an old established printing family, occupied an enormous flat on the ground floor. The managing editor of the *P.S.N.*, Jacques' fellow pupil in the Modern Sixth, had been given his parents' permission to have the exclusive use of a store-room at the back. The school newspaper took shape at odd times, between four walls struck with gaudy posters, on a long trestle table covered in a fine confusion of blocks and galley-proofs.

Charlie let them in. He was dark, plump and short-sighted.

'I was expecting you.' He grinned at the bold hunters of con-men. 'A good newspaper man has to put out feelers everywhere and I've had mine out twenty-four hours a day on the police-station in the Avenue de Paris. Now sit down and tell me the worst.'

In addition to Charlie, the editorial office of the *P.S.N.* contained a slender fair-haired girl of fourteen, his sister Lily, energetically bashing away at an ancient typewriter, and the unspeakable Patureau. Nicknamed Flatfoot, he was tall and thin, with a red face, an untidy mop of hair and the ability to earn more detention than anyone else in the Lycèe Alfred-Jarry. The school villain was simultaneously the paper's secretary, interviewer, photographer, sub-editor, artist, street-salesman, office boy and, at the end of the month, office cleaner as well.

The Thiriets responded with shy smiles and sat themselves in a row on the filthy old sofa pushed up against the wall. Jacques had filled two foolscap pages with an item-by-item account of the whole business. He launched straight into his essay, interrupted now and then by his younger brothers, who recalled the whirlwind preparations for the move, the splendid performance put on by the two confidence tricksters, and the unexpected appearance of a certain black cat. His voice stopped.

'Hurrah!' shouted Charlie, sending proofs flying in his enthusiasm. 'The *P.S.N.* has reached its hundredth issue and it's dying of the commonplace. Your story comes at just the right moment to get its circulation up again. Just think. We've a readership of three thousand half-wits all sleeping safe and comfortable and dreaming of the future. Most of them don't know what goes on around them. Now we've got a terrific story! Each one of them, as they read the tragic business, will feel part of it because it could happen to anyone . . . What an issue this'll be!'

Flatfoot waved his ham hands in disagreement.

'Steady on. I don't trust people who take all their ideas parrot-fashion. If we give them the story straight, like any other news item, they're going to have a high old time ragging the Thiriets and laughing at their father. So long as no one actually dies or gets crippled for life, most people find other people's misfortunes a grand joke. So your idea'll misfire completely. We've got to make three thousand dimwits in the Lycée Alfred-Jarry sit up and take notice with something genuinely mysterious. The Thiriet case is going to mean a lot more to them than the seventy-two points the basket-ball team scored last Saturday or the fact that Toto of Two B has a sister who's just married the Vicomte Lionel de Croquesoux de la Ville-Lanlaire!'

'But how are we going to put the thing across?' Charlie asked, his interest aroused.

'Dead easy! You ask your father to print two issues a week and we'll start a twenty-five part pre-publication serial of a thriller with a really good title like *The clue of the black cat*! We can't lose; the *P.S.N.*'ll sell like hot cakes!'

'Who's going to write it?'

'The three of us – and the Thiriets'll help. We'll have a pseudonym – Elsa Pristie – or MacFarlane or something, and to make it look more genuine we'll add: *translated from the English by Lily Baron.*'

'That's a splendid idea,' the managing editor exclaimed. 'But you've forgotten one thing – we've got the start of the story, but not the finish.'

'I know,' Flatfoot agreed with a wink. 'And that's the very

way we'll get our three thousand readers. The Thiriets' experiences will make up the first two episodes. Meanwhile now the investigation's opened all sorts of things may happen.'

'And what if they don't?' Jacques asked.

'Then we'll make them up ourselves, and we'll make them up so that we put the whole school off its food and sleep!'

The special issue of the *P.S.N.* came off the machines on Friday night and the first thing Saturday morning willing helpers were selling copies on the games-fields, in the playgrounds and dining-halls, and at the four entrances to the Lycée Alfred-Jarry. *The clue of the black cat – Part 1* filled the whole of the back page below an eye-catching title in thick black type. Flatfoot himself had drawn medallion portraits of the cat silhouetted in three attitudes – curled up in a ball asleep, surmounted by the question-mark of his long tail; springing at full stretch like a panther; and finally spitting with rage, all four legs stiff, his hair on end.

Charlie and his co-writers had transposed the names of people and places so that the whole story seemed fiction pure and simple. In this way the Thiriets had the pleasure of recognizing themselves without the pain of their class-mates' curiosity. They agreed that it kept pretty close to the truth, apart from slight exaggeration of detail in describing the slum in the Rue Mirandole, the ghastly privations of the family, and the precarious health of the cave-dwellers. The first episode ended on a note of breathless suspense as Peter Pancake (*alias* Bobby Thiriet) fitted the fake key into the door of the new flat, a key which would not turn.

At school, then, it was a runaway success and in some forms they even fought for possession of copies of the new issue of the *P.S.N.* The six conspirators met that evening after school in the dusty box-room that served as their headquarters, with mutual congratulation on this devastating kick-off.

'A lot of fellows bought two, and sometimes three copies for their parents and friends,' a triumphant Flatfoot announced. 'Even if we print five thousand copies of next

Tuesday's issue we won't be left with a single one unsold on our hands.'

'I'll tell Father,' Charlie Baron said. 'How did the readers react?'

'Not one of them has a clue,' Jacques roared with laughter. 'And the funny thing is that only a day or two ago there were a few lines about the real Thiriet case in the Paris newspapers. Everybody's forgotten it. They all gobble up the story of the fictional Pancakes and don't see any connection between the two families.'

'What about the second episode?' Laurent asked.

'Went to press last night so we're out of news. From now on we'll have to keep one jump ahead of events. Any news from the Rue Mirandole?'

'Not a thing,' Jacques confessed. 'The investigation gets nowhere. Dad is summoned to the police-station nearly every night to go through pile after pile of photographs. So far he hasn't set eyes on the White Hedgehog. On the other hand Commissioner Sinet keeps on at him for being so dumb. Apparently there's a law now by which he shouldn't have paid a sou for the Grand Duchess's carpet and cupboards until he'd had an expert valuation. It's the last straw! And now a couple of detective inspectors have been round at the house bombarding us with their stupid questions. They've been over in Fred's and up at the Belloy Private Estate as well. Then the Papadakis have laid charges, too. They noticed, a bit late in the day, that one or two things had vanished from their flat.'

Bobby seemed to be sulking in the corner, his head in a copy of the *P.S.N.*

'What's the matter?' Lily asked. 'Don't you like our serial? Charlie and Flatfoot really surpassed themselves.'

'The black cat only gets half a dozen lines,' the disappointed infant answered. That's not enough after the way he appeared on the scene of the crime and vanished as suddenly. You're like the cops, you won't take any notice of my evidence. If everyone makes that mistake your story'll just fizzle out, and so will the police investigation.'

Charlie picked a copy of the *P.S.N.* off the tablc and read out the passage at the top of his voice.

> '*Peter Pancake* (that's you) *halted abruptly at the door, his heart pounding. There, on the edge of the piano a huge black cat sat motionless as a statue glaring at him with eyes of flame. Overcoming his alarm Peter put out a hand to stroke the animal. It began to purr like a turbine. Just at that moment . . .*'

'There's no point in going on,' Bobby cut in. 'The black cat's left the stage and he isn't coming on again.'

'Don't worry!' Flatfoot reassured him. 'Your puss'll purr twice as loud in the next issue.'

'That's all very fine! But you might at least have put down that I was the only one who saw him in the Papadakis' flat that night.'

'At the point our serial and Commissioner Sinet's investigation have reached,' Charlie answered carefully, 'it's not an essential detail. We'll bring it in later on if we run out of copy or if the Sherlock Holmes of Puisay runs out of clues. Your black cat won't be lost to the world.'

His sensible remark concealed his own doubts and that made Bobby lose his temper.

'I didn't make it all up! When we went round the flat the first time there wasn't a sign of the beastly cat. It was only afterwards when the grown-ups were talking in the hall and I went off on my own that I found him making himself quite at home, sitting on a rosewood cabinet. Suddenly Daddy called me away and I just told him about the cat. I didn't think anything of it.'

'And then?'

'Everybody rushed into the drawing-room but the old devil had disappeared like magic.'

'You ought to have looked under the cabinet,' Laurent teased him.

Bobby shrugged.

'I would have done, only the old hag behaved as though I'd made it all up.'

'She was scared of something,' Lily Baron suggested. 'That's what you reckon?'

'Yes and no. She had a good laugh at the idea of a stray cat wandering about the empty flat. But what really seemed to annoy her was to be taken for one of those silly old women who've got nothing better to do all day long than make a fuss of a dog or a cat or a goldfish or a canary.'

Charlie whistled softly through pursed lips.

'Bobby,' he said at his most friendly, 'you're a darned sight cleverer than a professional detective. Your hunch leaves us gasping. We'll note it down for future reference. Even if we never catch her, that Grand Duchess has no fear of her luck going against her except of suddenly being exposed by a black cat with yellow eyes.'

The faithful Flatfoot had been folding, wrapping and addressing a copy of the *P.S.N.*

'I'm going to slip a copy into the letter box at the police-station,' he told the others. 'If the Great White Chief's asleep in his armchair, he's only to read our serial to start climbing up the wall.'

The following Tuesday the police investigation had still got no further. In the Lycée Alfred-Jarry the only event that grey day was the appearance of the *P.S.N.* with the second instalment of its thriller filling the last page – the Pancakes had let the tricksters get away with their savings and the black cat of the title sniggered into his whiskers.

For the last twenty-four hours budding stockbrokers had been running a book on the possible ways the needy family might survive. A goodly number of optimists had betted firmly on a happy ending and saw their pocket money vanish with the savings of the ill-housed Pancakes. Sensitive readers wandered round each form-room with long faces and little inclination either for work or play. Others tried to bribe Flat-foot to tell them what was going to happen next and ease their anxiety. How would the Pancakes get out of their difficulties? Would Inspector Mike Coogan ever catch the Grand Duchess and the White Hedgehog?

'You'll find out on Friday in our next issue,' the reporter from the *P.S.N.* told them. 'We know as much as you do on the paper. Elsa Pristie airmails her copy every two days. As the serial runs to twenty-five instalments and we've only got as far as the second you've plenty of time to let the excitement build up . . . You'll just have to lump it!'

In short, the five thousand copies went in one morning. Charlie and his general factotum sat mildly triumphant in the box-room on the Boulevard Champaubert. Neither of them showed the least anxiety about the failure of the police which automatically imperilled the serial, for the first two instalments had used all the source material provided by the Thiriets.

'Go home and don't worry,' they told the three brothers. 'Even if there's no fresh news by Thursday night, Friday's issue'll split the school from top to bottom.'

There were few smiles to lighten the gloomy evening in the basement of the Rue Mirandole. George and Sophie only half approved of the new page in the *P.S.N.*, for it seemed to make fun of their distress. The second instalment had the real-life ending with the Pancakes back in their hovel in Morton Street unpacking their bags, laid low by their disaster, but it finished on a note of suspense which was pure fiction.

Peter Pancake lay sobbing on his narrow couch when a stealthy sound jerked him up. He looked round and the hairs on his head stiffened – there against the skylight was the sphinx-like silhouette of the black cat, staring at him with its yellow eyes. (To be continued.)

'Too right,' Laurent judged. 'Flatfoot wasn't thinking and now he's gone and lumbered himself with this wretched cat. How on earth is Charlie going to work it all into the next instalment?'

'He had to keep his readers in a state of suspense,' Belle pleaded for him. 'It's a just a trick; it doesn't interfere with the author's real plan.'

'Okay, but why get away from the facts? Like it or not, that cat's going to end up by pushing us out of the picture and we'll be left with just any old pulp-magazine thriller.'

'All you've got to do is tell Charlie he's got to get rid of the cat in the next instalment,' Jacques suggested and laughed. 'Get him run over by a lorry, that'll do the trick. Flatfoot'll stuff the brute for you, free of charge. So that'll settle the cat's hash once and for all.'

Bobby said nothing. As he saw it the story could suddenly take any one of four or five turns. To his surprise, too, he had noticed that fiction was beginnning insistently to influence reality and oddly to weave itself into the pattern of his life.

A little later, when the lights were out and his elder brothers asleep in their bunks, Bobby sat up quietly in his camp bed and stared around in the darkness of their room. But the semi-circle of the skylight was empty.

At that moment in a new building on the Avenue de Paris a pale-faced man bent over his desk. Commissioner Sinet was busy reading the second instalment in the *P.S.N.* which, like its predecessor, had been sent to him by unknown hands. For him, too, fiction threatened dangerously to borrow the facts on which his investigation was based. On his side all trace of the crooks had been lost; they were still on the run, and, with no real clue to work on, he was in a fever to know how inspector Mike Coogan would extricate himself from a similar predicament in the third instalment from the villains of the Lycée Alfred-Jarry.

Sinet carefully folded his copy of the *P.S.N.* and slipped it into an inner pocket. He had just put on his overcoat when the telephone on his desk rang. It was Monsieur Breton, the ex-policeman caretaker of Block 6 on the Belloy Private Estate.

'I'm sorry to call you so late at night, but a funny thing's happened and I thought you ought to be told about it. That lad wasn't telling a tale the other night when he said there was a cat with the confidence-tricksters. Only a moment ago when I went down to the basement to see to the boilers the brute nipped out from under my toes. A fine black cat, it was!'
'What's so odd about that?' Sinet grumbled angrily. 'It was the Papadakis' cat . . .'

'It wasn't, you know. I took the lift straight up to the eighth floor and rang the bell. Madame Papadakis came to the door and what do you think I saw behind her? Why, her Toddles asleep in a chair.'

Sinet was left speechless.

'If you ask me,' the caretaker went on, 'our two birds left the old puss behind when they did their flit.'

'No proof of that!'

'Yes, there is. Since Madame Papadakis got back she's caught that stray two or three times in her kitchen. So he knows the place.'

'How does he get in?'

'Through the tradesman's entrance, on the heels of a

delivery man. Or maybe he slips in if the french window on to the balcony isn't shut properly.'

'But why the devil does he hang around the flats?'

'You know the saying–' Monsieur Breton laughed, 'you wouldn't put a cat out on a night like this!'

'That's no good reason,' bellowed Sinet, suddenly losing his temper.

'Well, simply suppose the owners are in the area as well, and the cat visits the Papadakis on his daily round. His real home may be in one of the neighbouring blocks. You think how the Belloy Private Estate has fifteen hundred flats – why, it's a little town of five or six thousand inhabitants all on its own. Two fly birds could easily hide out there under different names and, who knows, in a different disguise.'

Sinet would have had to rack his brains to get that answer. The black cat suddenly obsessed him.

'You've got to catch him!' he thundered.

'I'll try,' Monsieur Breton chuckled before he hung up, 'but it's not going to be easy.'

5
The trail of the black cat

THAT Friday, as three thousand boys converged from all directions, on foot or on bicycle, upon the Lycée Alfred-Jarry they shivered with cold as the first snow of an early winter drifted down. But Flatfoot and his salesmen soon warmed them up with the *P.S.N.* Two thousand copies went that morning at the four entrances to the school and the rest of the issue vanished in the first few seconds of the lunch break. Meanwhile even the dullest imagination had been fired by the transformation of Elsa Pristie's thriller. Excellent fellows, known to all for their stolidity and coolness, now went home with staring eyes, muttering darkly under their breath to the alarm of the passers-by. The young form-master of Two B nearly caused a riot when he confiscated a copy of the *P.S.N.* passing between the desks at the back of the class-room. However, the storm was hushed when they saw him enthralled by the back page – *The clue of the black cat.*

The title was there sure enough, but the rest of the page was startlingly different both in content and in lay-out, which copied the editorial arrangement a daily paper sometimes makes when it has a real scoop.

Charlie started the firework display with a leader in heavy type which filled the top half of the page.

The time has come for us to take our readers into our confidence. The Pancakes and their four children, Sybil, Herbert, Sam and Peter, are no mere creatures of our imagination. The three boys are your school-mates at the Lycée Alfred-Jarry. They are perhaps in your form, you may even be sitting next to them. We have exposed their distress in all its nakedness and you have taken this courageous family to your hearts. Do not withdraw your sympathy from Jacques, Laurent and Bobby Thiriet. They belong to us, they are part of our daily lives. Their sad misfortune is true in every detail as you have read it in the two instalments of Elsa Pristie's *thriller.*

Do you want to know what is going to happen next? This depends upon your own reactions and upon what is going on in the unknown world around us. It is up to you alone to discover this and to bring the story to a happy ending. The thriller has gripped you. We are going to continue it together, but now it will be the real thing, and you will find it much more exciting than our humble serial. You yourselves will bring fresh life to the plot, you will be responsible for the startling revelations and for the breathtaking suspense.

What, then, is at stake? This is not only a matter of hunting down two crooks and making them disgorge their ill-gotten gains. This is but part of the game, the sporting side of the case which will put us in direct competition with the police. For us, big and small, the heart of the matter is to help friends who have been cruelly hurt and who have not deserved this blow of fate.

The clue of the black cat *will be the name of the investigations campaign your paper has launched. Read your* P.S.N. *carefully. We call upon your initiative and your ability to pick up the scent and stick to it. Success, we are sure, will crown our joint efforts. Thank you. Good luck and good hunting!*

Flatfoot and Lily Baron had surpassed themselves in the design and lay-out of the page. A précis of the facts of the case was followed by a detailed note on those actually engaged in its solution. Then, under the headline *What are the police doing?* Charlie pulled out all the stops once more to emphasize how slight were the clues so far gathered, to hint at a number of unexplored lines of inquiry open to amateur detectives, and to deplore the gradual slow-down of the official investigation. Under the heading *Housing and crime!* Jacques Thiriet had filled the two left-hand columns with extracts from the Paris papers, a sort of confidence trickster's roll of honour for the week, chosen by an expert in their effects.

This masterly lay-out led the reader straight on to the leading question: *Do you know these two? If so, tell us at once! If not – find them!* And there were two detailed drawings of the Grand Duchess and the White Hedgehog. These identi-kit portraits had come from Flatfoot's pencil after hours of work with Bobby Thiriet, the only one of the brothers to have seen the originals close up in the Papadakis' flat.

The lower left-hand corner was kept for important instructions: *If you discover anything, write, telephone or come to the office of the paper,* 12 Boulevard Champaubert, *any evening between six and eight,* Charlie had advised, forgetting how small those offices were. While the sales manager announced: *No* P.S.N. *is wasted. Read it! Re-read it! Lend it to your friends in Paris! Send it to your friends in the country and abroad! Your copy may fall into the hands of someone with the information to set us on the track of these crooks.*

The lower right-hand corner was the black cat's kingdom. There he sat on his haunches, his whiskers on end, a thoughtful attitude which matched his imaginary statement that surrounded him.

I alone know who the Grand Duchess and the White Hedgehog really are, he had been made to say. *I spent several days in a stranger's flat in which these crooks had made themselves at home to plunder the poor. I'm only a black cat like thou-*

sands of others, but if you should happen to come across me, I shall lead you straight to the gentleman who poses as a public benefactor and to the lady who denied my existence to Bobby Thiriet's face.

That evening the hall of Number 12, Boulevard Champaubert had never been so full of people and the caretaker was hard pressed to control the stream of rowdy schoolboys who poured in endlessly, shouting and slamming the doors. From the very beginning there was a concerted rush on the offices of the *P.S.N.* and Charlie found himself suddenly swamped by the wave of enthusiasm which he, in his scepticism, had aroused.

Luckily it did not take Flatfoot long to restore order. He made them all wait in a long queue which stretched right down to the cellar. The visitors were then allowed, six at a time, into the cramped box-room where the managing editor dominated proceedings from behind his desk, his sister-cum-secretary on one side, the Thiriet brothers on the other. The latter were stared at as though they were freaks in a side-show. Lily took down any definite information as it was revealed, and then there would be a round-table conference to consider, with becoming gravity, the importance and the use to which such scraps of news could be put. At length the informant would depart in the happy assurance that his name would be in the next issue of the *P.S.N.*

On several occasions the meeting was nearly broken up by practical-joking infiltrators. Needless to say they themselves were the only ones to snigger at their own stupidities.

'We're not here for fun!' Charlie would bellow from behind his desk, his finger pointing at the culprit. 'I know who you are. Your name's Grosmalin. Your parents live in an eight-room flat on the Avenue de Paris. Would you like Jacques Thiriet to take your place there? You can take his for a day or two in the basement in the Rue Mirandole. We bet it won't take you long to see things a bit differently.'

The joker tiptoed out, but Commissioner Charlie's office was not completely bereft of its lighter moments. The evidence of certain simple souls was sometimes on the level of a knockabout farce, though given with complete sincerity. Typical of them was a young hobbledehoy of Two B called Poussard. He arrived muffled to the eyebrows in a hooded cloak covered with snow.

'I know that one!' he announced in a snuffling voice as he pointed to a sketch cut from the *P.S.N*.

This was the first direct evidence to come before the meeting.

'You know the White Hedgehog?' Charlie frowned.

'Course I do. Your artist didn't half make a good job of him. He didn't get his lines crossed.'

Flatfoot took the compliment sceptically. There were about a dozen really hard cases in the Lycée Alfred-Jarry, and Poussard was one of the hardest.

'You really know what you're talking about?' Charlie could not believe his ears. 'If you're going to identify somebody with absolute certainty you need more than a passing glimpse of him in the street.'

Poussard's round eyes flashed from under his hood.

'For the whole term,' he said bitterly, 'I've been seeing your White Hedgehog full face, sideways on, and rear view – so put *that* in your pipe and smoke it!'

'Who is he?'

'Old Freckleface of course!' Poussard exclaimed, furious that the others should have missed something so obvious.

'Who's Freckleface?' Charlie bellowed, and banged the table.

Poussard looked pityingly at the committee and waved Flatfoot's sketch in front of them.

'Really!' he said in tones of deep disappointment. 'Can't you see who it is? Monsieur Vacherin – our Maths master!'

A moment's bewildered silence greeted his revelation and then there was a gale of laughter in which Poussard, who was pleased with the expected outcome, himself joined. When all was quiet once more in the box-room he remarked, 'Well, wasn't I right?'

'I've got to admit there is a likeness,' Charlie agreed. 'But what shakes me is that no one noticed it this morning, not even our talented artist, when nearly everyone had a copy of the *P.S.N.*'

Flatfoot rubbed his ham-like hands and rejoiced.

'At last we've got a suspect to go on our list.'

'Why not?' said one of the boys waiting his turn at the far end of the room. 'There's nothing to clear Monsieur Vacherin so far.'

Lily wrote his name down and turned to the other members of the committee.

'What are we going to do?'

Charlie and Jacques shrugged uncertainly. Laurent kept the joke going.

'Let's appoint Poussard official investigator in Two B,' he suggested with a perfectly straight face. 'He can confront Vacherin in the middle of the class and ask him if he has an alibi for the hours of six to eight on the evenings of 26th and 27th November. With thirty kids hanging on his slightest reaction, if he is guilty he'll be out of the front door like a greyhound out of the trap.'

'And if he's not guilty?' asked Flatfoot.

'Then Poussard's career as a detective'll come to an abrupt end with a couple of clips to the head!'

'You don't really mean that do you?' Charlie's question was lost in general laughter.

The voice of reason sounded from the darkest corner of

the box-room where Bobby had been patiently holding his peace for the last half-hour.

'Monsieur Vacherin's nothing like the White Hedgehog,' his treble cut across the argument. 'I'm the only one of you who's actually seen the con-man to talk to and heard his voice. Anyway, you can bet the masters at the Lycée Alfred-Jarry aren't paid enough to be able to afford the sort of blue overcoat our public benefactor was wearing.'

They patted Poussard on the back and sent him on his way. He might only have been trying to pay off old scores, but they could use his information all right. It would make an amusing paragraph in the next issue of the *P.S.N.* There was more laughter before they got down to work again and Bobby took advantage of the hubbub to slip discreetly out in the wake of Poussard's hooded cloak.

All along the Avenue de Paris the shop windows sparkled like a firework display in the dark and the snow which heralded Christmas, now three weeks away. Commissioner Sinet, his hat pulled down over his eyes, shoved his way through the loitering throng on the left-hand pavement. Aware of the excitement in the air, he cursed his profession which unfairly kept him busy while so many others strolled along thinking of the presents they were going to give and those they would be given. Of course he could have passed the job on to the dimmest of his inspectors at the station, but Sinet wanted to keep the business in his own hands. They'd been laughing at him behind his back for too long now.

He cut down the Rue Pochet which brought him out on to the Boulevard Champaubert. His right hand thrust in his overcoat pocket automatically fingered the copy of the *P.S.N.* that had come by the morning's post. To his regret Inspector Mike Coogan seemed to have left the stage for good, but the kids who ran the paper had put their cards on the table. Sinet now saw himself ideally placed to use to the full any clues which were of real importance, despite the light-hearted way in which they were presented. 'What's the point of endlessly poking and prying, cross-questioning and shadowing people through the suburban mazes that will one day be Paris?' he said to himself. 'The little fools have come into the case of their own free will and they'll work like demons to solve it. They really are keen to get on the right track. Luckily they're slaves to the school time-table so they won't be able to follow it quickly or right to the end. Then I shall step in and finish the job. But I shan't do the dirty on them and take all the credit. It doesn't worry me whether *France Soir* mentions the Commissioner from Puisay or not; I'll be certain to have my photograph at the head of a three-column interview in the *P.S.N.*!'

The closer he approached the park the wider were the gaps between the fine new buildings on the Boulevard Champaubert, each block of flats surrounded by snowcovered gardens that glittered in the lamp-light. As Sinet passed Number 12 he noticed through the tall glass doors a youthful crowd coming and going in the hall. 'Another night on the tiles,' he thought disdainfully, 'but the black cat won't be joining them.' By now he could see on the far side of the square the eight tall towers of the Belloy Private Estate soaring through a shifting curtain of snow towards the sky.

Muffled in a fur-collared jacket, Monsieur Breton paced up and down outside his lodge. Above him, balconies shimmered in the light of a thousand windows. People were coming home. Every few seconds a car would sweep round the circular driveway to find its place in the inner car park or to plunge with headlights blazing down the ramp into the garage.

'Where is he?' Sinet asked casually.

'Shut in the basement. He could have got through to Block 5 if I hadn't lowered the metal curtain between the two garages, but as the skylights have all been shut for the night the only way he can get out is up the service staircase. The door's behind the lift shaft. I'll show you.'

Somewhat abashed, Sinet followed him into the hall. People were passing hither and thither calling greetings as they met. Monsieur Breton drew him to one side and pulled a key out of his pocket.

'There's the door!' he said and pointed to an oak panel with a round red light above it. 'If we open, he'll just as easily slip between our legs and vanish into that mob. If you're dead set on nabbing him, the hunt'll take us up to midnight and he won't be the first to tire . . . So what are we going to do?'

'Leave me the key, and push off home,' Sinet answered grumpily. 'Once the crowd thins out I'll open the door and wait. We'll see what happens then.'

Five minutes later, through the north door from the square came Bobby. He strolled along with a carefree expression on his face as confidently as if he had been scuffling the muddy cobble-stones of the Rue Mirandole. His chubby face was almost lost in the hood of his duffle-coat. He shook himself like a penguin before he went in, to get rid of the layer of snow that covered him. Then he glanced through the glass doors and down the hall. He saw the door gaping open on the black patch of basement just as he spotted Commissioner Sinet's figure at his post beside the lift. Fortunately the policeman had his back to him.

Bobby withdrew into the darkness, circled the block and came through the south door from the car park, on the heels of a gentleman who had just locked up his car. Sinet was out of sight, so he hid behind the curve of the main stairs to the right. Soon it would be eight o'clock. There were fewer and fewer people about and the lifts were out of use for long periods.

Sinet stood stock still in his corner sucking on a dead pipe as he waited. Never for a moment did his eyes leave the open doorway a little to his left, almost within his arm's reach. The hall remained quiet. The black cat chose this moment to make his slow, sure-footed entry, one ear cocked for the subdued hum that came from the floors above. The first thing Sinet saw was his head with his shivering whiskers, then came his glistening furry body and then his tail whipping to and fro anxiously. Reassured, at last the cat stretched and then sat down. Calmly and carefully, he gave himself a wash and brush-up, licking his paws to clean behind the ears. He was beginning to purr happily when he sensed the close presence of a stranger. He gathered himself, the fur rising along his spine.

Sinet did not stir, and at last the black cat's head turned and his glowing eyes fell upon the motionless man concealed in the shadows. For a moment they looked at one another without daring to breathe. 'The brute's going to give me the slip,' the policeman said to himself and got ready for violent action. But the cat wanted to make friends. To his astonishment Sinet could hear that purring which seemed to say 'Stroke me!' Sinet made a friendly sound and the cat approached him timidly, one foot at a time, his belly brushing the floor. Gradually his back arched as he came nearer and nearer and then he gently rubbed himself against the policeman's legs. Never in his life had Sinet won the confidence of a living thing, and he was overwhelmed by this instinctive trust so freely given. The cat mewed and returned to the attack, but could not move the man so sadly rooted to the wall. In the end he tired of the lack of response and, whirling round, his tail lashing, he was across the hall in a flash.

Bobby from his corner saw him swish past and vanish up the stairs. He waited a bit longer. Soon, the dark shape of the policeman came out into the lights of the hall and with immense precaution ascended the first flight of stairs. Bobby gave them twenty seconds' start and then tiptoed up after them. The policeman was tailing the black cat and Bobby was tailing the policeman. Slowly the three companions passed from floor to floor with many a delay as the cat sniffed at a doorway, stopped to scratch behind the ears, turned in his tracks or froze at the sound of the lift-gates slamming. Commissioner Sinet did not attempt to rush him, remaining respectfully in the rear for fear of frightening the animal. Bobby got the rhythm of their slow progress as he flattened himself against the wall, peering out to look up and then pulling back at once if he saw the policeman only just ahead.

On the eighth floor there was a fresh delay while the cat had another wash and brush-up. With three corridors to choose from, he trotted down the left-hand one. Sinet only followed him half-way before he hid in a doorway to watch what would happen. Bobby meanwhile waited on the top step ready for a rapid withdrawal should the policeman turn round. Several seconds passed before the mew of the cat filled the end of the corridor with its dirge.

Sinet, his interest aroused, leaned out and looked down the corridor. Bobby took advantage of this to make up ten or twelve yards of ground, and flattened himself in the next doorway.

The black cat was rolling ecstatically on the end doormat, mewing and scratching the closed door which filled the long perspective of the passage – Flat 121!

6

The clarinettist

A CLOCK in one of the flats struck eight. Monsieur Breton had promised to help the Commissioner's investigation by not turning on the automatic time switch for the corridor lights. However, he must have forgotten all about it, for now every one went out. All that were left were the red and green lift indicators vaguely illuming the head of the stairs. Bobby stared into the darkness and listened. The black cat mewed more loudly and at last the door opened, sending a beam of light sweeping across the passage. Silhouetted against the brightness was the figure of Madame Papadakis bent over the purring cat.

'Has he come back zen, ze naughty ickle sief!' she chirruped. 'Come in zen oo wicked! Come zay hullo to Toddles!'

She opened the door still wider and there, like a fat black ball, on the carpet in the hall lay the other cat. The visitor hopped inside and at once the door closed, plunging the corridor in darkness. Quite near him Bobby could hear the Commissioner grunting and swearing under his breath. He was about to make a tiptoe escape when from the ground floor came the sound of voices and instantly the lights snapped on. Two somewhat sheepish detectives stood blinking face to face in the brightness. Sinet muttered an apology as he brushed past the small duffle-coated figure standing sentry outside Flat 125. He paid little attention to him until, reaching the head of the stairs, something clicked in his brain and he slowly retraced his steps.

'Haven't I seen you somewhere before?' he asked curiously.

Bobby was quite unconcerned.

'I was in your office at the police-station the other evening.'

Then Sinet recognized the round and grinning face in the hood of the duffle-coat. At once his suspicions were aroused.

'What are you looking for?'

'The same as you,' Bobby retorted. 'And we've just both proved that there really are two cats round the place. So I wasn't making my one up.'

'Granted,' Sinet sighed grudgingly.

'Pity he can't talk!' Bobby added as though to himself. 'He'd tell us all sorts of interesting things about those two crooks and what they've been up to.'

The Commissioner's eyebrows shot up. The kid seemed to be underlining the subtly-phrased caption to the picture of the cat on the back page of the latest issue of the *P.S.N.*

'Like playing detectives?' he asked roughly.

'No, I don't! But just you remember my father's ten thousand francs vanished in this block of flats and whatever the caretaker may say, I think that pays my entrance fee all right!'

Sinet was moved by the counter-attack which so clearly showed the boy's feelings.

'Well, don't let's argue,' he said in a gentler voice. 'Are you pleased to see that the Commissioner's taken personal charge of shadowing your black cat?'

'I couldn't believe my eyes,' Bobby answered. 'Your stock went up a hundred points between the ground floor and the eighth!'

'Honoured!' Sinet bowed.

They both laughed and this sealed their alliance. All the time they had been talking the lights in the corridor had remained on. Monsieur Breton had at last remembered his promise. Sinet pointed to the door of the Papadakis' flat.

'Admit it, you don't trust them?'

Bobby was only too ready to air his views.

'Just because there are two cats doesn't let them out. On the contrary it only makes them stronger suspects in another way. A stray cat doesn't make friends with any old one. And their story of a trip seems pretty fishy to me. I'm not accusing anyone, but if one of these fine days, they're found to be hand in glove with the two crooks, I shan't fall over backwards with surprise.'

'But Natasha Popov's little stay cost them a packet,' Sinet objected. 'Two fur coats, a rouleau of gold Napoleons and all the family silver!'

'They don't seem very upset about it,' Bobby answered with a grin. 'Anyway not enough to bar the Grand Duchess's cat from the house.'

Silence fell. The lift had just stopped at the eighth floor. Out into the brighter light at the stair-head stepped a young man in a camel coat with a Robin Hood hat on his head. In his hand he held a long clarinet case in black imitation leather. Sinet and Bobby turned and watched him vanish down the centre corridor.

The Commissioner still grunted and then he pulled the *P.S.N.* out of his pocket and opened it at the back page. Bobby noticed that he had pencilled a blue ring round the picture of the black cat and the caption under it.

'If this issue ever gets into the hands of our two birds,' Sinet said slowly, 'they won't waste much time trying to get their cat back.'

'The Grand Duchess didn't seem all that fond of him,' Bobby answered dubiously.

'She'll change her mind sooner or later and so will her accomplice.'

Bobby pretended to be very astonished.

'Why?'

'Their finger prints are no good to us – Records have nothing on them – so there's only the cat. He doesn't seem to worry about being left in the lurch. But your paper puts words into his mouth that carry a hidden meaning. It's quite right, the police could use the cat to track down the confidence tricksters. So in a way puss is as good as telling them, if they can read between the lines, "Come and get me while there's still time." Maybe one day we'll see them shove their noses into Block 6. We'll be waiting for them when they come out. Monsieur Breton's been warned and he'll let us know the moment he has any suspicious visitors.'

'I'm glad to hear that,' Bobby said politely.

'You never guessed as much when you read your *P.S.N.*?'

'Of course I did! The black cat's my pigeon on the paper. I'm the one who has to write the copy for him. I never thought the police would cotton on so quickly!'

Sinet flushed and glared at him.

'You're not taking the mickey, are you?'

'I'd never dare!' Bobby protested. 'We're pals in fair or foul.'

Sinet screwed up a smile.

'I'll believe you. Now, let's go shall we?'

But Bobby did not move.

'We ought to catch the cat right away,' he said gravely. 'That trap you were talking about just now is going to work a jolly sight better if we've made sure of the bait.'

'What are you worried about?'

'The black cat, our one, could get tired of the Papadakis and leave the building for good and all.'

Sinet scratched his head.

'I'd like to have a shot but it's not going to be all that easy. The caretaker says that cat's a real devil . . . Got your running legs on tonight?'

'I'd start by making friends with him,' said Bobby. 'I wouldn't worry him. I'm too small to scare him.'

'He might let you stroke him a bit. But he'd never let you collar him.'

'Let's try, anyway!'

Sinet was delighted to play a game which would set him on an equal footing with a mischievous schoolboy.

'Good,' he said. 'You carry on. Ring the Papadakis' bell, ask them for a bit of string, catch the animal and put it on a lead. But for Heaven's sake, my lad, make sure you've got the right cat!'

'What about you?'

'Don't worry. I'll be ready behind you.'

Bobby liked the plan. Nonetheless he was most anxious to test the Commissioner's good faith.

'I'd rather you made the first move,' he said. 'The Papadakis'll remember me from last time and slam the door in my face. But they wouldn't dare do that to someone like you!'

'And if the black cat gets away between my legs?'

'I'll be behind you to catch him. Nothing'll make me let go!'

Sinet exploded.

'No! No! And no again! You'll drive me mad with all you're asking me to do.'

He nearly pulled off his black hat and hurled it to the ground in rage, as in those days of the Horse Without a Head and the Street Musician. But a ghostly hand restrained him. It belonged to another Sinet who had never enjoyed the happy childhood of his fellows and who still felt he had a claim to those lost years. From then on all was changed. The responsibilities that had overwhelmed him a moment before suddenly lightened. Yes, the chief editor of the *P.S.N.* had been quite right to make a breathless twenty-five part serial out of a dull little incident which already gathered dust in the police-station files.

With a harsh movement Sinet tightened the belt of his overcoat to give himself courage.

'Come on!' he said gaily. 'We want that cat and we're going to get it!'

'You're a smasher!' Bobby whispered.

They reached the door of the flat. Sinet rang, once, twice, three times. Nothing happened and he began to hammer on the door. The fearless Bobby retired a step or two and took up a good position to catch the cat in full flight. An angry voice sounded from the other side of the door.

'Open in the name of the Law!' called Sinet, forgetting that the summons had no legal force after sunset.

Nonetheless Madame Papadakis did open the door very, very slowly. She stiffened at the sight of the chief of police of Puisay.

'What do you want?'

'I've come for the black cat,' Sinet answered gruffly. 'I don't want any trouble, just hand him over, in a basket, preferably . . .'

'Have you gone out of your mind?' Madame Papadakis, getting angry, tried to shut the door. 'Arrest a cat!'

But Sinet put a foot in the doorway.

'I'm not talking about your Toddles. I want the stray you let into your flat at eight o'clock exactly. I was at my post in the corridor and I saw him go in.'

They did not hear Monsieur Papadakis coming. He was wearing carpet-slippers and carried a newspaper.

'Really! What are the police coming to?' he said cuttingly. 'The two cats are eating their fish in the kitchen. Do you want to question them?'

'Keep your cat but give me your guest at once!' bellowed Sinet. 'Or else you and your whole Zoo'll have to come with me.'

His warning echoed through the flat. He had not even time

to close his mouth before the black cat rocketed over his right shoulder and landed in the middle of the corridor. Bobby was crouched all ready, but the brute slipped between his outstretched arms and vanished in three jumps down the stair-

case. The Papadakis' door was slammed in the detectives' faces.

Bobby seemed delighted by their raid, but Sinet looked very depressed.

'I knew we'd never hold him. You saw! Down eight flights like a flash and now he's hiding in the basement. If Monsieur

Breton can't catch him a clout with his shovel we'll never get him!'

'Why are you so set against him?' Bobby asked quietly. 'The poor old thing's caught up in this topsy-turvy business just like we are. He's got a right to live.'

They had reached the lifts at the head of the stairs from which three corridors led, when they noticed the clarinettist standing expectantly outside an obstinately closed door. There was something unnatural in his tense attitude. Sinet felt himself on the attack, master of all in this new block of flats which might well shelter a pair of crooks.

'What the devil are you doing hanging around the place with that musical instrument?' he growled.

'I'd arranged to meet the Wild Cats of Puisay,' bleated the musician with an idiotic grin. 'We were going to run through Art Tatum's "I've found a new cat". But they aren't here yet and I'm beginning to get worried.'

'Well, for the neighbours' sake, I hope you've got the wrong address. Go downstairs and ask the caretaker. It's far too late to play clarinets round the place.'

Ignoring the lift conveniently on their floor, Sinet, wishing to get all the fun he could from their meeting, led Bobby downstairs.

'Don't worry, boy!' he said with real friendliness. 'We'll get that thieving hypocrite your poor father thought was such a good kind man.'

'The *P.S.N.*'ll help you twice a week,' Bobby promised frankly. 'Only do tell your men to leave us a bit of elbow room. My friends won't harm a soul when they're working for a good cause like this.'

When they reached the ground floor Sinet glanced at his watch and at once grew anxious.

'Won't they be waiting for you at home?'

'I shan't be last in,' Bobby assured him.

'Monsieur Breton'll get me a taxi and I'll drop you at the corner of the Rue Mirandole.'

Five minutes later they were there. But by now the Commissioner's failure was beginning to rankle.

'I'll be dreaming of that black cat half the night. We'd almost got him! You shouldn't have let him escape.'

'I never thought he'd be so quick. But hasn't one thing struck you – that stray knows his way round that huge block of flats like his own back-yard.'

Sinet shrugged without answering. Luckily Bobby remembered Charlie's watchword – you've got to keep the reader interested, no matter how. Life was like an adventure story; the time was ripe and he gently turned the page.

'The black cat told me something as he slipped through my fingers.'

They had got out of the taxi and the snow whirled gently round them. Sinet stared into the ingenuous face framed by its hood, smiling up at him.

'You aren't pulling my leg?'

'You agree,' Bobby calmly explained, 'that there were two black cats in the Papadakis' flat?'

'I saw them both,' Sinet admitted. 'And one plus one makes two.'

'Even close to,' Bobby went on, 'you can't tell the difference between them. All the same I knew mine at once.'

'Which?'

'The crooks' cat, of course. The one who was sitting on the cabinet like a stuffed animal the night of our first visit with the White Hedgehog.'

'How did you know?'

'I should have remembered earlier. Round his neck he's got a thin, thin chain. You can hardly see it his fur's so long. Madame Papadakis' Toddles hasn't anything like that as I discovered the second time I was there and I stroked him.'

'That all?' asked a bewildered Sinet.

'No,' Bobby answered. 'At the end of the chain there's a disc, about the size of a thumb-nail. I tried to pull it off, but the tiger-cat got away!'

7
Stop press

On Saturday evening from four o'clock, the office in the Boulevard Champaubert never emptied and Flatfoot had to joke and clown to keep the waiting queue in the corridor happy. Lily Baron's post was at the telephone in the flat, where she jotted down any news coming to the paper. Every so often she would push through the crowd in the box-room to cast a handful of scribbled notes on the managing editor's desk. The latter never stopped his joint cross-examination, with Jacques Thiriet, of the investigators and witnesses who had flocked in from every corner of the town. In view of the amount of information and the successful investigations made that very morning among the various forms in the Lyceé, Charlie was able to open proceedings with a shattering announcement.

'We're bringing out the *Puisay Students' Sunday News* tomorrow morning! Four pages devoted exclusively to the black cat! The first three set up already and we're holding up the stop press until the end of the evening for Flatfoot to beat it hotfoot to the printers! I've made room for some good big headlines, but I've got to fill the page with something sensational and I hope one of you waiting will bring me it while there's still time to print it . . .'

There were as many jokers in this Saturday crowd as there had been the day before, but as many showed a shrewdness astonishing for boys of their age. A friend of Laurent's, called Belmont, a weedy boy with brown hair and dreamy eyes, absolutely useless at all games, particularly interested the committee.

'I've nothing much for you,' he said modestly, 'it's just

something that struck me yesterday evening after I'd read the account of the business in the *P.S.N.* It's this: was it just by chance that the White Hedgehog was in Fred's barber shop on the same evening as Bobby and his father? I don't think it was . . .'

'What do you mean?' Charlie asked.

'The way the confidence trick was worked shows that it had all been planned beforehand and wasn't just to catch the first person who came along.'

'It *seemed* a chance meeting,' said Jacques. 'Bobby's no slouch and if there had been any funny business at all at Fred's he'd have spotted it.'

'Your successful con-man is successful just because he can engineer events to make them look like pure chance. It's the best way of inspiring his victim's trust. I'm sticking to my guns: someone knew Monsieur Thiriet's difficulties, and it looks as though he'd found out all about his time-table, too.'

Belmont had made a point and his statement brought a hush to the box-room.

'It's something to think about,' said Jacques. 'In any case, the policemen who came to our place to make inquiries were on that tack, but they didn't follow it up.'

One question led to another.

'Outside the family,' Belmont went on, 'just who could have known your father was going to Fred's place on that particular evening?'

'First of all, Fred himself!' Jacques said and looked surprised. 'Dad had been round the evening before to fix an appointment . . .'

'Who else?'

'Maybe the office manager at Rouillon's, the Estate Agents. Dad went to look over a flat for sale with him in the afternoon and he may have just mentioned he was going to Fred's before he left him.'

'Anyone else?'

Jacques laughed and nodded.

'Monsieur Luret, the landlord of Number 33, Rue Mirandole. His flat's right above ours so he can easily spy on all we say and do.'

'The old boy may not be exactly a pleasant customer,' Laurent agreed, 'but I'd be very surprised if he makes a bit on the side by tipping off con-men.'

'We'll put him on the list of suspects all the same,' Charlie decided. 'And the others, too. We'll have to detail two volunteers to keep an eye on Rouillon's. We need another one to have a haircut at Fred's. The paper'll pay. It's just a reconnaissance flight. Who'll go?'

Laurent stuck his hand up.

'I'm ripe,' he said ruffling a thick mop of hair. 'And anyway Monsieur Fred doesn't know me, so he won't be suspicious.'

'Want to go right away?'

'Yes, but the place might be jam-packed.'

'All the better. Sit down, pick up a paper and keep your eyes and ears open while you wait your turn.'

'Right. Give me the money.'

'Go up to the flat. Lily'll give you enough for a hair-cut and the tip.'

'What about a shampoo?' Laurent asked. 'If something did turn up, a shampoo might give me five precious extra minutes.'

'All right then; hair-cut and shampoo – but that's all.'

Laurent went out grinning all over his face as he struggled into the blue anorak which had already served two winters on the burly shoulders of Jacques. Charlie meanwhile returned to Belmont.

'Well done. We'll hold on to your theory. It'll make a half column in the "stop press". Of course we shan't name any

names. We don't want the first issue of the *Sunday News* to land us in a libel action! . . . Now who's next?' he asked the waiting crowd.

The red face of Flatfoot the doorman peered round the half-open door.

'There's a lady,' he hissed. 'She looks about seventy so I didn't want to keep her waiting with the others on the cellar steps.'

'Show the old girl in!' Charlie sighed – nothing could surprise him now.

The twelve boys who filled the box-room rose as one when their visitor appeared. She was a little old lady, bent and wrinkled, dressed all in black, carrying a heavy shopping bag and an umbrella that dripped melting snow. Her lips were pursed in a sharp smile. The idlers who had slumped down on the battered old sofa got clumsily to their feet to give it up to her. She thanked them as she sat down, her eyes flickering inquisitively over the boys big and small who looked at her as though she had come out of the Ark.

'You're all like a lot of cats,' she told them with a tinkling laugh. 'I know all about those rogues, but you can take it as a compliment. My name is Madame Deuzy and I live at the end of the Rue Pochet and I'm eighty. I'm a regular reader of your *P.S.N.* because of that black cat, of course, the one that's causing you all this fuss. My neighbour's little grandson lent me your last three numbers. You want people to help you and, as a matter of fact, I've something very interesting to tell you . . .'

'It was very kind of you to have come in spite of the weather,' said Charlie, trying to keep a straight face. 'Why, you wouldn't turn a dog out on a night like this.'

'Snow's just as bad for cats as it is for dogs,' Madame Deuzy retorted, rather shocked.

She took from her shopping bag a copy of the last issue of

the *P.S.N.* open at the page on which was the picture of the Grand Duchess.

'I know the woman you're looking for so hard,' she said, her finger jabbing the paper. 'So I dropped everything to come and tell you, because I dislike her as much as you do.'

This was far beyond Charlie's wildest dreams. Professional confidence tricksters adopt a hundred different disguises, have a hundred undiscoverable retreats, and their shadowy, fugitive existence leaves a rapidly vanishing track on the scene of their crimes.

'Who is she?'

His question boomed like a gong in the hushed atmosphere of the box-room. But the old lady was quite unperturbed.

'Your Grand Duchess's real name is Madame Papadakis. She lives in Flat 121, Block 6 on the Belloy Private Estate . . .'

'You're mistaken,' Jacques Thiriet told her quietly. 'Madame Papadakis is a perfectly respectable lady. The police have cleared her of all suspicion. Why, she herself has suffered through employing that scheming creature.'

'I'm positive of what I'm saying,' the old lady went on. 'I had tea with Madame Papadakis in her flat on the 25th of November in the afternoon. That's the day before Monsieur Thiriet and his little boy went round to see her with that diabolical White Hedgehog.'

'No,' Charlie said patiently, 'you're forgetting the Papadakis were still away then. The person who really let you into Flat 121 was the former housekeeper, Natasha Popov, who had taken the place over with her accomplice. The Grand Duchess bears no physical resemblance to the real owner.'

'But I can't be wrong,' Madame Deuzy protested. 'It was the third time I'd met Madame Papadakis and that fraud of a woman hadn't changed in the meantime.'

Charlie and his amateur detectives were very worried by

this. Her evidence revived the suspicion nurtured originally by the police themselves, that the owners of the flat were involved in the plot. Belmont, on the point of leaving, stayed to listen to what was coming.

Charlie would not be put out of his stride.

'Where and when did you first meet Madame Papadakis?' he quietly asked the old lady.

'It was last spring.' Madame Deuzy had regained her original smile. 'I was trying to find a home for my Toddles, a fine young black cat, five months old, but so greedy and sly and lazy that it would have to be with somebody well-off. (When you've lived with cats as long as I have there are things you get to know straight away, and I've still to make a mistake.) So I put an advertisement in *The Puisay Municipal Echo*. Two days later this Madame Papadakis rang me up to say she'd give the orphan a home. "I should so like to have a black cat," she told me. "If your Toddles is house-trained I'll take him sight unseen. My house-keeper will be round in a few minutes with a nice new basket." A few moments later into my flat came a hoity-toity creature in a fur coat, the very one your artist made such a good picture of in the latest *P.S.N.* "I'm Madame Papadakis," she says all la-di-da. "I thought I'd better come myself. Where's the cat?" I showed her Toddles. She hardly looked at him. Popped him in her basket and out she goes without so much as a thank-you or telling me where she lives. I ran out to call her back but her taxi was disappearing round the corner of the Rue Pochet . . .'

Charlie interrupted her apologetically.

'You were dealing with Natasha Popov, the housekeeper, although you didn't realize it at the time. Madame Papadakis said Natasha was always borrowing her fur coat and pretending to be her.'

Madame Deuzy's little black eyes flashed.

'I know what I'm talking about,' she retorted. 'I spent six

months trying to find out where that cat-thief lived. But I had no luck until the beginning of last week, when who should I see in the market on the Avenue de Paris? Why, the cause of all the trouble strutting along on her high heels as proud as a peacock in her fur coat. I didn't waste a moment.

' "I've got you now! You won't get away this time! What have you done with Toddles?"

'She pretended to be surprised to begin with.

' "Who's Toddles?"

' "The black cat you stole from me . . ."

'She remembered then and began to look very awkward.

' "I'd forgotten all about it," she said with a sickly grin. "Yes, yes, Toddles is splendid. But I've given him a new name. He's called Sasha now."

'There was something so suspicious about her that I wanted to get to the bottom of it.

' "I want to see him," I told her. "When I give a cat away, it still somehow belongs to me because I've been responsible for finding it a home. I'm only a poor old woman but don't you try to slip off again. I've a long arm where cats are concerned."

'Madame Papadakis seemed very frightened and even more embarrassed by the crowd who were listening to us. They know me and if I'd shouted "Stop her!" the stuck-up thing would have had a score of people on her tracks. All her fine airs disappeared and she calmed down.'

'You may not know it,' said Jacques Thiriet admiringly, 'but you really put her on the spot.'

'That's what I thought,' the old lady admitted. 'She looked quite bewildered. I didn't beat about the bush. 'I want to see Toddles," I insisted. "Where do you live?" She went white as a sheet at my simple question, and started to stutter. If you'd asked anyone there they'd have told you she had something on her conscience. Suddenly I felt somebody pluck at my elbow. I turned and there was the errand boy from that big baker's shop, Sautereau's.

' "Don't you let her get away with it," he whispered. "I know her. She's the worst payer in the neighbourhood."

' "Where does she live?" I asked.

' "On the Belloy Private Estate: Block 6, Flat 121 . . ."

'Now I'd got Madame Papadakis.

' "I'm coming to see you this afternoon," I told her firmly. "If I find the door shut or if you won't show me Toddles, you won't hear the last of it. I shall go straight to the police-station and tell my story to the Commissioner." '

Jacques, Charlie and their friend Belmont listened without showing the amazement they felt at the energy of the frail Madame Deuzy. Six months before, the Grand Duchess's conceited pretence to be the mistress of the house who went out so seldom, had taken in plenty of people. But at the very moment when the absence of the Papadakis made her position doubly secure, it had only needed a meeting with this old lady to imperil the whole plot. And this had happened on the eve of the master stroke in the trap-flat. On the other hand, since Toddles was away with the real Papadakis, the crafty investigators of the *P.S.N.* at last perceived the tips of the ears of black cat number two, whose presence had at first seemed so inexplicable.

'And so,' Charlie asked with bated breath, 'you went round to see her that afternoon?'

'Of course I did! I'd hardly rung the bell before Madame Papadakis opened the door, full of apologies for our little misunderstanding that morning. She even had a cup of tea for me.'

'And was the cat there?' asked Jacques.

'I saw Toddles. That fool of a woman, can you imagine it, had re-named him Sasha.'

'You're sure it was the cat you'd trained yourself?'

The old lady appeared genuinely astonished.

'Toddles had grown a lot in the meantime,' she admitted, 'but he seemed to know me and he was very friendly. There he was living like a king in that lovely flat. Well, to cut a long story short, I left quite reassured, and told Madame Papadakis she should be careful not to give him too much milk or sweet things.'

She finished speaking and smiled at the friendly faces which surrounded her. Charlie made not the slightest attempt to explain to her how she had confused the real Madame Papadakis with the adventuress and her Toddles with another black cat brought in from the outside. This heaven-sent misunderstanding was all to the advantage of their investigation. In any case the dear old lady had something much more serious on her mind.

'I hope that thieving woman goes to prison,' she said as she picked up her umbrella and her shopping bag. 'But I don't want poor Toddles turned out into the street. When the confidence tricksters are arrested, arrange for the innocent creature to be brought round to me.'

'Don't you worry,' Charlie reassured her. 'He's in good hands at the moment.'

He helped her up and politely escorted her to the door.

'I'm so glad I came,' she remarked as she was saying goodbye. 'You're good lads. I was afraid I'd find a lot of nasty practical jokers.'

'The pleasure's been all ours,' Charlie assured her with a bow, 'and you'll have no cause to regret your visit. The story you have just told us is worth a life subscription to the *P.S.N.* To show our thanks we shall be sending you a free copy of every issue throughout each school year to come.'

She went out delighted, leaving the older boys agog with her evidence. Charlie at once sat down at his typewriter.

'Here's to the old girl! Thank heavens for her!' he shouted. 'She's given me half the copy for the stop-press page. I'll knock something together that'll be worth another thousand on the circulation of the *P.S.N.*'

Belmont was still standing beside the door.

'And don't forget,' he murmured, 'that the old dear has explained in a couple of sentences just why the crooks lumbered themselves with a second black cat. Imagine the panic the Grand Duchess must have felt to find her secret threatened by the vengeance of a casual passer-by. She could have ruined all their best-laid schemes! Why, I can hear her phoning the Hedgehog for a black cat there and then. "I've got to have one this afternoon or we're sunk! That old witch'll rouse the neighbours and fix us for good! . . ." And then our public benefactor worked like crazy to find a cat in time. No mangy brute, but a plump well-behaved puss to fit Toddles's description. If he shanghaied one from some other suburb we're doomed to reach a dead-end – black cats aren't exactly rare, you can pick one up on any street corner.'

'As far as we're concerned,' said Jacques, 'the main thing is that we can lay our hands on the crooks' black cat. From the last we heard, he hadn't left the Belloy Private Estate. He seems to like it there. So long as he doesn't give us the slip we've got them by the slenderest thread . . .'

'I hope someone's looking after it?'

'Bobby's there this evening as usual. The black cat's his baby.'

Charlie, his head in his hands, racked his brains over the lay-out and the stop press.

'Time's getting on and I still haven't a headline yet . . .'

He swung abruptly to the visitors lounging on the moth-eaten sofa.

'Come on, you dozy individuals! Give me some ideas! Four or five words for a headline! Something short and snappy with a real punch . . .'

One of the idlers raised a flabby hand.

'Why not make something up?' he said lazily.

'That's all very well,' growled Charlie, 'but what?'

'BLACK CAT MURDERED!' the idler answered, stressing every syllable.

There was a hush in the box-room. Charlie removed his glasses and stared short-sightedly round at them all.

'But it won't be true when we go to press,' he said in some embarrassment.

'A good journalist isn't as fussy as that,' sniggered the other. 'And then a spot of blood on the front page'll stir Puisay up nicely.'

Silence fell one more. The managing editor replaced his glasses and scribbled away nervously. The fat black capitals neatly filled the space. Jacques was looking over his shoulder.

'You're going a bit far,' he said, somewhat shocked.

The other waited without daring to breathe. A moment's thought and then Charlie hammered the table with his fist.

'We'll kill the black cat!' he bellowed, 'and bring him to life again the next issue on Tuesday. Someone get me Flatfoot and tell him I want twenty-five lines on the murder with no names mentioned. It's terrific! What's more, the false news'll make a first-rate trap for the crooks – they'll think they've got the brute off their necks . . . BLACK CAT MURDERED!' he bellowed again and sent the papers flying ceiling high.

Jacques got to his feet and buttoned his coat, unaffected by the general excitement.

'Disapprove?' Charlie called as he went.

'Not a bit. Just going to see how the cat is and let Bobby know at the same time. He'll think your news a great joke . . .'

8

The death of the black cat

IN the last few days Bobby had grown bolder. Now he walked round the Belloy Private Estate as though it were some overgrown village. Lost in the throng, he had nothing to fear from the caretakers. The ground floor tradesmen's entrance gave directly into the hall and through this covered way, with its glittering walls of glass and its hurrying crowd of busy people, you could enter the heart of each block without the slightest risk.

He got there at ten past four, the hood of his duffle coat pulled down to his eyes, his hands deep in its pockets. A fine snow had been falling all day and mantling the distant prospects of the new town where the lights twinkled in the dusk. On the Estate the upper storeys vanished like mountain peaks behind the thick curtain of flakes.

As he came in through the tradesmen's entrance Bobby glanced at once to the left of the lifts. The basement door was shut and there was no sign of the gloomy form of Commissioner Sinet. How far could he trust him? At any moment another important case might crop up somewhere else in Puisay and draw him away from the trail of the black cat, with the result that, if the crooks lived locally, they would be left quietly to dispose of the Thiriet family's ten thousand francs.

Looking quite unconcerned, Bobby stepped across to the door to try the handle. It would not give. On his way back past the lifts he suddenly noticed among the waiting throng a ludicrous figure which seemed vaguely familiar. It was the musician of the night before in his camel-hair coat, his Robin Hood hat with the cock's feather, hugging his clarinet case under his arm, waiting among the rest for the lift that served the central wing. Bobby paused for a moment, staring ahead. He now felt he had seen this peculiar person somewhere other than on the Belloy Private Estate – but where?

Commissioner Sinet's hand was heavy on his shoulder.

'Been here long?'

The smile on the long swarthy face was as friendly as it had been the night before.

'Not much more than five minutes,' Bobby answered. 'I meant to wait for you down below, as we'd arranged, but the door's locked tight shut.'

'Monsieur Breton did that, and I expect you can guess why. The black cat spent all the morning rollicking round the top of the building and then came down for a warm up in his favourite spot – next to the boilers. I'd rather have it this way. We shan't have to knock up the Papadakis and have all that fuss all over again. And in the basement, with the three of us, we should be able to catch him in the end.'

'Perhaps we won't need so many,' said Bobby. 'If you leave things to me, he'll come of his own accord.'

'Like last night,' Sinet joked. 'If the black cat's in a bad mood, we'll have our hands full ... Ah, here's Monsieur Breton.'

The ex-policeman barely acknowledged Bobby's greeting, but shook the Commissioner warmly by the hand. Then he unlocked the basement door and all three went down the concrete steps to the first cellar. One end was filled by the mass of boilers and the oil storage tanks. Opposite was the shaft of the service lift, the garages, now shut off by the lowered metal curtain and then the narrow passage leading to the individual cellars and ending in a blank wall. The black cat's kingdom was thus sealed off on all sides.

'He ought to be over there!' Monsieur Breton called and pointed vaguely towards the boilers. 'Catch him as quick as you can. This part of the basement can't be shut up for more than an hour or two, and once you've got him I want to open the skylights and the garage shutters . . .'

The red flame of the boilers, filtering through the cracks, flickered in the darkness and sent the shadows dancing on the long bare walls. The roar of the burners filled the basement and muffled all other sound. Bobby had halted behind the two men, his eyes searching in every twilit nook and cranny for a slinking black shape.

'A hundred watt bulb in the ceiling,' Monsieur Breton went on in answer to the Commissioner's question. 'I'd like to turn it on but it'd scare the cat and you'd have ten times more trouble delivering the K.O.'

He was the only one to brandish a broom handle, and Bobby was grateful to Sinet for coming empty-handed like himself. The policeman made a sign and Bobby moved over to the boilers on his left while the former went behind the storage tanks. Monsieur Breton remained in the open space between them and the garage.

The closer he got to the boilers, the more deafening was their roar and the heat was almost unbearable. Bobby loped along peering into every cranny and narrow gap between the metal casings. The black cat was not far away, crouched motionless in one of these cavities. The boy could not even make out the shape of his eyes, but guessed he was there from the fleeting red reflection of the fire in his eyes. Realizing it had been observed, the cat squeezed itself even further down the narrow gut. Meanwhile Commissioner Sinet had inspected the tanks and, as he came up to Bobby, he flashed the beam of his torch from side to side.

'Seen anything?' he called.

Quickly Bobby weighed the pros and cons. The balance was tipped by his sudden fear of the savage glee of the hunters and the terror of their prey trapped in the black and oily hole.

Turning to Sinet he merely shrugged and shook his head perplexedly.

Luckily the Commissioner did not bother to make a closer inspection and the black cat was saved by his own silence and stillness.

'Search the passage to the separate cellars,' Monsieur Breton advised them. 'That's the only place the confounded creature can be. If it gives you the slip, let me know and I'll have my broom-handle ready for it on the way out!'

He flicked a switch at the foot of the stairs and a dozen dusty bulbs lit the main passage from which several other dead-ends led. They explored this area without success. If only the cat will stay put! Bobby thought as he pretended to search with great zeal. This was less to deceive Sinet than to spare their wretched prey the fate in store for it.

'Still no sign of him,' Sinet said, as they returned to the foot of the stairs. 'Are you sure you closed everything properly behind you?'

'The cat was there right enough, sitting in front of the service lift when I locked the basement door,' the caretaker assured him.

He switched on the ceiling light. The whole basement was lit by the glare of the bulb. Bobby waited with bated breath, but the black devil had the sense to stay put. To salve his conscience Sinet decided upon one final search of the tanks and boilers.

'Could you let me have your broom handle?' he asked the caretaker. 'If the cat jumps out on me I'll lay him cold.'

Purposely Bobby passed first before the narrow cavity now full in the glare of the light bulb. To his intense surprise the cat had vanished, nor did Sinet find him on his side. At first the boy doubted whether he had really seen him a few minutes before. But no! The pair of eyes he had seen glitter in the darkness had indeed belonged to the black cat.

'Let's take a look upstairs,' a thoroughly bad-tempered Sinet grumbled. 'Open up if you've got to, and leave the door on the stairs ajar. He'll come back for a warm by the boilers . . .'

He and Bobby alone went up the stairs, leaving Monsieur Breton to open the skylights and to send the iron shutters to the garage up with a tremendous clatter.

'Your black cat's pulling a fast one on us,' the policeman said angrily. 'Now, come clean, were you making up that story of a chain and medal you told me?'

'They were there last night! Didn't you hear them clink when he darted between us? If he lets us get anywhere near him, we'll have his name and address.'

With a sweeping gesture Sinet opened the door.

'After you, sonny,' he said kindly.

At that moment they heard a cry from Monsieur Breton in the basement. The black cat was hot on their tracks. It came leaping up the stairs to take the lead, brushing past the Commissioner in its hurry. Landing on the tiles of the hall it shot through the startled crowd there. A few small boys, shrieking with delight, joined in the fun of the chase. The black cat dashed for the staircase.

As his paws bit the treads the lift on the left shot up for the eighth floor with one passenger on board – the clarinettist, his case clasped under his right arm. With only his muscles to drive him up the stairs, the black cat just beat the lift. He was down the end of the left-hand corridor in a flash, scratching at the door of Flat 121 and mewing at the top of his voice. But tonight no one opened the door.

Back up the corridor turned the black cat, and then suddenly the fur rose on his spine. The eighth floor landing was deserted, but slowly and threateningly the door of the lift slid open. There stood the clarinettist, his left foot holding the gate back while with frantic haste he opened his case and produced a long gleaming instrument which no more resembled a clarinet than a saucepan does a violin. Nothing stirred. The clarinet came up to his shoulder. He took careful aim. The black cat might have been a rabbit at twenty paces. Two shots rang out.

The first buzzed angrily like a wasp past the black cat's ear, the second caught him without warning full in the ribs. He collapsed on the Papadakis' door-mat, clawing the air. The satisfied marksman packed his gun away at once, propped open the gates of the lift with the case, and sprinted down the corridor. The black cat no longer twitched. Judging that all was up with him, like the fox in the fable, he shammed dead. His executioner's hand ruffled his gleaming fur and with one jerk broke the thin chain and snatched with it the paltry aluminium disc.

The two shots had sounded just like a firework. Christmas was on the way and nobody on the ground floor took a scrap of notice. Sinet and Bobby were waiting by the left-hand lift. The red light on the indicator panel winked to show it was coming down and they bumped into the clarinettist as he came out, his case clutched to his chest. 'Him again!' the Commissioner growled. He was beginning to grow curious at the way their paths kept crossing.

On the eighth floor a dozen doors were ajar and people were talking nervously and glancing over their shoulders. Sinet jumped.

'Rifle shots? Don't talk nonsense . . .'

They hurried to the Papadaki's flat. The black cat had vanished but a trail of blood showed where he had gone. They found his limp body half-way down the stairs. Commissioner Sinet had changes sides in the last twenty-four hours and the murder of the black cat made him far angrier than the disappearance of its disc.

'Don't worry, Bobby! I'll catch the killer and he'll play a different tune on his clarinet.'

Bobby was very stiff as he fought back his tears, standing beside the body of the animal. A moment later he had taken off his duffle coat, folded it, and into the bed thus formed, had, with infinite care, laid the body of the black cat.

'Do you think he's dead?' he whispered.

'Of course not! Cats have nine lives!'

'I'm taking him home and as long as he's got half a one left I'm going to nurse him.'

Below, the throng in the hall was as thick as ever and no one paid any attention to a sad-faced little boy walking behind a tall, horse-faced gentleman. As they pushed open the tall glass outer doors, they ran full tilt into the eldest Thiriet. Jacques had no qualms as he came with the false news from the *P.S.N.* He turned quite pale when he saw what Bobby was carrying cradled in his arms.

'Is he dead?' he asked and gently stroked the limp body.

'Not quite! We'll find out when we get him home . . .'

A faint mew came from the bundle of black fur Bobby was protecting from the snow. Sinet was touched by the sorrow of the two boys. They had lost so much, but still kept the better part of their pity for an animal in pain.

'I'll take you home in a taxi.' There was a catch in his voice. 'Leave the rest to me. We'll be on the hunt till two in the morning at the station – and we won't have clarinet accompaniment!'

Jacques got them to drop him off at Number 12, Boulevard Champaubert.

In the editorial box-room there was just a cheerful half-dozen round a gay, untidy Charlie. They turned as they felt the blast of cold air from outside.

'Come in or get out, but shut the door, you idiot!'

Jacques stood motionless in the doorway gazing at the boys who had greeted him so heartily. When the noise had died down he gasped into the silence, 'The black cat . . . murdered!'

His friends doubled up with laughter.

'Stale news!' said Charlie coldly. 'The last batch of copy's just left and the *Sunday News*'ll be off the press by midnight. I hope you haven't been running to and fro confirming false information.'

Speechless Jacques slowly extended his right arm and showed them a blood-stained hand. Charlie understood at once and bounced up from behind his desk like a jack-in-the-box.

'Catch Flatfoot!' he shouted at his assistants. 'Knock him down and kill him if you have to, but bring me back that stack of drivel he unloaded on us . . .'

9
A gentleman called Dupont

LAURENT quietly waited his turn in the barber's shop. He watched the faces around him and, since the misfortunes of his family had not made him very tolerant, in his eyes each newcomer assumed the appearance of a thief or a degenerate. The youngest of the six assistants was missing, Monsieur Fred's nephew who lent a hand on busy evenings. He crept in towards seven, a long black, imitation leather case under his right arm. The ever-smiling Monsieur Fred, who was artfully arranging the three remaining hairs of some elderly hopeful, turned and snapped his scissors.

'Here comes our Gaston,' he laughed. 'Late as usual ... Well, how did the rehearsal go?'

'My clarinet played like a dream,' the young man assured him.

He went to the staff room and came back almost at once buttoning up his long white coat. When he had disposed of a bald-headed gentleman, Laurent was the next to entrust his hair to the temporary barber. One word led to another and soon they were discussing jazz, twist and rock. In the end all the cash advanced by the *P.S.N.* was exhausted. Was it money down the drain? All seemed open and above board in the luxurious saloon through which passed the cream of Puisay, diluted occasionally by some shabby or simple-minded individual to whom the handsome Monsieur Fred showed the greater consideration in view of his very obvious embarrassment.

Laurent got back to the box-room at about half past seven to find the atmosphere had changed. Only Belmont, Flatfoot and the eldest Thiriet remained, talking seriously to a now grave, unsmiling Charlie. Lily was back in her corner hammering madly at a battered typewriter. Briefed by Commissioner Sinet and by Bobby, Jacques had just given an unvarnished account of what had taken place some forty minutes before at the Belloy Private Estate. Now he had all the facts, the managing editor thought he had given their essentials in his stop-press.

'Now they've pulled this off,' he was telling the others wearily, 'the crooks have got clean away. We'll never catch them.'

Nobody took any notice when Laurent came in wafting a smell of hair-oil, except his elder brother.

'Two hours for a hair cut,' he said bitterly, 'I hope you had time to probe about a bit.'

'Couldn't see anything odd,' Laurent admitted, somewhat sheepishly. 'The place was packed when I got there.'

'A good spy never hangs around a crowded place,' Charlie said dryly. 'You could have slipped out after half-an-hour.'

'One of the assistants was missing. The one who helps out on Saturday afternoons. I wanted to take a look at him at all costs.'

'Well?'

'This fellow Gaston – he's a keen jazz man – came sweeping in around seven.'

'Where'd he sprung from–' Belmont asked, surprised. 'A hairdresser's assistant doesn't just disappear on a Saturday evening.'

'He'd been playing his clarinet on the other side of Puisay,' Laurent answered with a broad grin. 'The fellow belongs to a local group called – just listen to this – the Wild Cats of Puisay.'

Lily stopped typing. The others looked at one another wild-eyed. Charlie rose abruptly to his feet and snatched his wind-cheater from the back of the chair.

'Let's see the Great White Chief!'

Sitting in his office on the first floor, Sinet heard the racket made by a squadron of motor scooters sweeping down the Avenue de Paris at top speed. The new patrol had gone out on the beat and there were not many policemen left in the station. Nonetheless Sinet rang down to the duty officer.

'Send out the squad car and pull those yobbos in! Keep them inside for two or three hours, that'll cool them down a bit. If we let them carry on Puisay'll be like the Wild West in six months . . .'

But the police had no need to take action, for the detectives of the *P.S.N.* came sweeping into the station, calling for the Commissioner at the tops of their voices. Without waiting to be asked, the five boys swarmed up to the first floor and burst into Sinet's office, an unfortunate duty constable clinging to their elbows.

They waved their arms, stamped their feet, shouted and shadow-boxed, all talking at once as if they were in the Parrot House in the Zoo.

'Shame! Shame! . . . The Black cat's killer walks the streets with his clarinet! . . . Fred shelters gangsters and nobody cares! . . . The poor are robbed, cats and dogs are killed and they get away with it, soon they'll be on to the kids and the grannies! . . . Do something! . . . Put that scum inside and be quick about it! . . . There're plenty of passengers for the black maria! . . . Arrest the lot! . . . The staff of Rouillon's Estate Agency, and the Papadakis, too! . . . They're bound to be in it!'

Sinet raised his arms despairingly and at last the hubbub died down. It had all been carefully rehearsed by Charlie who wanted to press home his viewpoint by speaking first. The Commissioner defended himself manfully.

'You're all crazy! I can't shove twenty people inside on some trivial charge. That would be just too easy. First of all you've got to open the case, cross-question the witnesses, put the suspects under observation . . .'

'And in the meantime,' Jacques said bitterly, 'the White Hedgehog's parading the Grand Duchess round all the night clubs and making hay with Father's money.'

Then Charlie interrupted to give a detailed account of all that had been said and done since four o'clock in the editorial offices of the *P.S.N.* Thanks to Belmont's subtle deductions, to the old lady's visit, and to the individual activities of the Thiriet brothers, the newspaper's investigations had advanced in a definite direction and the net had closed a little tighter round the guilty ones. But what, meanwhile, had police headquarters been doing?

'Don't accuse the police of sitting back and doing nothing,' Sinet replied. 'We've been on another tack which brings us just as close to the crooks, and no stone's been left unturned in our investigation of the activities of the most minor characters in this affair. Why, for the last two days I've had one of my plain-clothes men round at Rouillon's Agency in the hope that another mug to con might draw the White Hedgehog out. Then we know minute by minute what the Papadakis are doing. We've had their telephone tapped. In just the same way Monsieur Fred's hairdressing saloon is under close watch. A few minutes ago Laurent Thiriet had his hair cut, but he never knew that the man on his right was a police inspector who also noted the late arrival of Monsieur Gaston and his clarinet.'

'What's stopping you arresting him, then?' Charlie shouted furiously.

'What use would that be? No one's laid information and the only charge you could bring is the very minor one of shooting the cat. I should have to let him go. Anyway, the cat's disc won't have stayed long in his pocket.'

Shyly Belmont raised a hand to ask if he could say something.

'There is someone you hardly seem to have thought of,' he said blushing. 'And yet he could fill in his piece of the puzzle . . .'

The Commissioner frowned.

'Who do you mean?'

'I think I'm right in saying that the White Hedgehog borrowed the identity and the visiting cards of a man called Henri Dupont to help him gain his victim's confidence. Now I know there must be a couple of hundred thousand Duponts in the Paris area alone and it would be a tough job for the investigation to sort out the right one. All the same, don't you think it would have been a good thing to concentrate on him?'

There was a smile on the Commissioner's long face.

'Excellent suggestion! The Dupont you mention is sitting over there, right behind you.'

Charlie and his friends had been beautifully caught. They turned abruptly to find an old gentleman in a black suit sitting peacefully on the visitor's seat in the darkest corner of the room. In the button-hole of his overcoat was the red rosette of the Legion of Honour. He waved an ironic welcome to the boys and then heaved himself to his feet with the help of his stick.

'The police,' Sinet went on coldly, 'try as far as possible to shield the names of respectable people who chance to be involved in unsavoury matters. The press generally follows the same course, provided their readers' passionate curiosity doesn't demand the very opposite. Applying this to the White Hedgehog's latest success, it means that Monsieur Dupont's name need only be mentioned once, at the beginning of the case. The *P.S.N.* has shown itself worthy of the best traditions by copying this policy.'

'I'm very grateful to it,' said Monsieur Dupont, limping over to the boys.

He halted in front of them and stared, with no hint of unfriendliness, into their tense, bewildered faces. Charlie was the first to regain his self-possession.

'Commissioner Sinet enjoys keeping us in suspense,' he laughed. 'You're the only one with the key to the mystery.'

Monsieur Dupont pretended to be extremely surprised.

'What makes you think there's a mystery in this sorry business? A con-man comes, and goes, that's all.'

He spoke as if it were a trifling affair, and this annoyed Jacques.

'My father looks on it a bit differently,' he said in an angry voice. 'The song my brothers and I hear every evening in our charming little hovel in the Rue Mirandole is "Oh where, oh where have my ten thousand francs gone?" '

Although Commissioner Sinet felt the same, he was careful not to say as much in front of his visitor. Someone so wealthy and so influential had a very long arm indeed. But Charlie had one thing on his mind and would not be side-tracked. He pulled a copy of the *P.S.N.* out of his pocket and stuck it in front of Monsieur Dupont. His finger was on the picture of the White Hedgehog.

'Do you know that man? He must have come in close contact with you, and not so long ago, to have had the idea of borrowing your identity.'

'I know him by sight and I know him by name,' the managing director of Metropolitan Properties replied.

'Who is he?'

He seemed much amused by the boys' anxiety. None of the five, however, noticed the sneer on the face of Commissioner Sinet as he leaned back in his chair and slowly filled his pipe. To rouse them still further Monsieur Dupont delayed his answer.

'The con-man's name is Papadakis,' he said at last. 'I've only ever met him once, last month at a cocktail party. We had a long conversation and exchanged cards. There was something suspicious about his – he must have got hold of it at another party – so I tore it up as I left. As for mine, well, you know the use he put it to, a fortnight later.'

Jacques and Laurent bowed in defeat. Once again the White Hedgehog had slipped through their fingers and this time it seemed for good. Commissioner Sinet rose from behind his desk and watched the group over the flame of the match with which he lit his pipe.

'Come on! Don't give up hope,' he murmured. 'We've still got the black cat.'

Charlie thought he was laughing at them. But, glancing at him out of the corner of his eye, he saw that the policeman was not fooling and that the 'we' he had just used meant he was still behind them.

The respectable Monsieur Dupont realized he was out of the running and silently stole away. No one saw him go.

Wearily and thoughtfully Sinet paced the office and puffed his pipe. As he did so he took the rough which Charlie offered him and cast an astonished eye on the *Sunday News*. There was nothing to which he could take exception. It was all in the honest, straightforward, somewhat simple tradition of reporting which lives on in provincial newspapers. But the chief editor's bold corrections told already of the need to startle the reader by dressing up the naked truth.

'Young Bobby keeps his eyes open!' Sinet suddenly addressed the gloomy group. 'He noticed the cat was quite at home on the Private Estate. The crooks are probably closer than we think . . .'

Laurent laughed bitterly.

'I gave up my half-holiday to hawk raffle tickets round the Estate, block by block and floor by floor. The boldest cop would have given up half-way. I didn't sell a single ticket and what I think of the generosity of Puisay people's too strong for even the Sisters of Mercy to change. My little stroll did make me sure of one thing, though – the Duchess and the Hedgehog are nowhere there.'

Commissioner Sinet's remark had struck ground in Belmont's fertile imagination.

'Bobby's the only one of us who really knows this mystery cat,' he told the others. 'Agreed it feels at home on the Belloy Private estate, but its instincts could be deceived by its surroundings. In other words, it thinks it's at home because its home surroundings are exactly the same.'

The idea had already crossed Sinet's mind. He had not dared pursue it, for thirty years in the Force had only served to strengthen his tenacious hold on the wrong theory, and boys who were too clever rather put him off.

Charlie shook his head and picked up his papers.

'I'll put another six lines in the stop-press. We don't want to miss a thing!'

'Why worry?' sighed Flatfoot. 'The black cat's probably dead by now anyway . . .'

But the black cat was still alive at midnight in the damp basement on the Rue Mirandole. Bobby had sworn to stay awake, but the excitements of the evening were too much for him in the end. He woke again at two in the morning and his hand groped over the end of his bed for the large cardboard box which Sophie Thiriet and Belle had stuffed with old rags to make a comfortable nest.

Bobby had a terrible fright when he touched it and found it icy cold. He sat up in bed, his eyes striving to pierce the gloom. Above him Jacques and Laurent whimpered like tired puppies in their sleep. The white curtain between them and Belle fell straight and unwrinkled to the floor.

Bobby turned to stare at the semi-circular skylight at the

other end of their cubby-hole. A bluish light, the dim reflection of stars and snow, filled the barred recess. There in the embrasure sat the still figure of the black cat high above this flat he found so strange. Every now and then his head would duck smoothly and he would carefully lick the wound in his chest. Then his eyes glowed red as he stared in Bobby's direction.

Bobby respected his independence and went to sleep again with his mind at rest. All was well. Flatfoot had only been anticipating reality by a few days when, in the last lines of the second instalment, he had described the arrival of the cat in the Thiriets' home. But the real excitement was not in the printed page which made the boneheaded idiots of the Lycée Alfred-Jarry laugh. The real excitement came from taking part in the real-life adventure of ordinary affairs.

10

Sunday News

THE first Sunday issue of the *P.S.N.* came out as planned and was busily hawked round Puisay by Flatfoot and his lads. They spent a wildly exciting morning. Charlie had replaced the headline that announced so definitely the death of their mascot, with a dramatic question by which his five thousand readers' imaginations were just as powerfully disturbed.

ATTEMPT ON BLACK CAT

WILL HE SURVIVE HIS WOUNDS?

(full details in the Stop Press)

There was a short summary of the lighning chase from floor to floor of Block 6 in which the killer, a local thug with a stocking mask, had hunted the animal to the end of a passage and shot it with his .22. Riddled by the bullets, the poor cat was dying in the home of his well-wishers in the Rue Mirandole. No clues had been found at the scene of the ambush, but the murderer had left his signature upon the crime . . .

The *P.S.N.* was hawked and sold down the Avenue de Paris and the neighbouring streets, in the two markets, in front of St Ursula's (by permission of the parish priest), in cafés, at the bus station – everywhere! Some newspaper kiosks even offered to take a hundred, and cleared their stock by noon. Of course the police had their copies first – and free. Sinet was wandering round his bachelor flat when he suddenly saw the *Sunday News* slide under his door. He dashed across and flung it open, but the news-boy had vanished down the stairs. The

Commissioner barely glanced at the headlines before fastening at once upon the stop-press. Charlie had kept his word. The black cat was there drawn in a typically crouching attitude with his tail swirling into a question mark above him. His deathbed message was his own way of putting across the theory of a cunning young man called Belmont.

The Belloy Private Estate seemed like home, but it wasn't really. I had only been transplanted from one place to another. Last night a stranger took it upon himself to remind me by playing me a little tune on his clarinet. It brought me within an ace of death. Will I recover? If you want the latest bulletin, see my friend Bobby, 33 Rue Mirandole.

Sinet thought the piece first-rate and his gloomy face brightened. He rummaged in his book-case, unfolded a map of the southern suburbs of Paris, and spread it on the carpet. In the middle of the sheet was the mushroom town of Puisay, while Sceaux, Bagneux, Antony and Rungis were shown as well. Armed with ruler and compasses the Great White Chief lay down on his stomach and went gravely to work at the map. The Belloy Private Estate was the fixed point from which he had to trace, in one or more directions, the route a cat could take and the distance it could walk in one day.

Outside it was very cold. The wind had changed in the night and there were large patches of blue sky beyond the clouds. The sun barely pierced through to glitter on the frozen crust of snow. From time to time groups of warmly-clad boys would turn the corner of the Rue Mirandole and look for the gloomy doorway of Number 33. Belle and her mother guarded the door of their cramped apartment to turn away their visitors without disappointing them. Yes, the black cat was doing fine. He had quite got over the .22 bullet and was now convalescing on half-a-pound of cod, the gift of the editorial staff of the *P.S.N.* A score of keen supporters, in fact, surrounded the three brothers and encouraged the animal's appetite. George Thiriet was out. He was doing Sunday duty at the Prochimac Laboratories at full overtime rates. It was tough, but at all costs he had gradually to make good the terrible drain on the family savings caused by the Duchess and the Hedgehog.

In the forefront knelt camera-reporter Flatfoot, his Rolleiflex focused on the black cat valiantly plying its jaws. One after another he took his shots of the victim pushing back the cod.

'What a cat!' Laurent said proudly. 'Got him smack in the ribs. Bullet's still there. Here! If you stroke his left side you can feel it under the skin.'

Hangers-on were pitilessly sent about their business by a frowning Bobby. The black cat, meanwhile, had disposed of the cod – they had wisely removed skin and bones, a bullet was quite enough – and now he was offered a saucer of fresh cream which he cleared in twenty seconds. Whereupon the noble creature curled himself up in his cardboard box and went blissfully to sleep. His audience tiptoed out, their minds at rest.

Commissioner Sinet did not dare come until early afternoon. The neighbouring streets were nearly deserted that cold Sunday. Nonetheless, as he got closer to the Rue Mirandole he noticed several watchers in blue, black or red anoraks posted here and there to form a ring of sentries round Number 33. There was nothing suspicious or threatening about them, but he preferred to keep well away and await events.

About two o'clock the black cat woke up and at once showed abnormal signs of activity for one so severely wounded. Up on to the ledge of the skylight he jumped, sat for a moment for a careful wash and then stretched himself gently to see that his limbs were in working order. Apparently content with the results of the test, he began at once to scratch at the glass which lay between him and the open air. Not one of the six boys in the little room moved, so he turned and mewed at them crossly.

'He wants to go out,' said Belmont. 'That's plain . . .'

'Shall we let him?' asked Laurent, glancing at his two brothers.

Bobby rose angrily to his patient's defence.

'You're crazy! The frost'll kill him stone dead.'

'He won't catch cold with all that fur,' Charlie chuckled. 'He just wants to stretch his paws. What's your worry? He's lost too much blood to keep going all the way back to the Belloy Private Estate.'

'If we let him out,' Belmont went on, 'maybe he'll go somewhere else. Closer to, or further away. Anyway we'll escort

him at a safe distance. If he starts to peg out, the Thiriets can just pop him back in his box.'

Bobby let himself be persuaded in the end.

'Get on your scooter and collect a dozen of the fellows,' Charlie told Flatfoot. 'Fix it up so they're positioned in sight of one another from the cross-roads. Jacques and I'll nip round the house. We'll keep an eye on the path beside the embankment. Let's hope the cat doesn't stick his nose on to the motorway.'

Ten minutes later the watchers were stamping their feet at their posts round Number 33. Bobby had been left alone with the angrily mewing cat to await the signal to let him

go. Soon Charlie's fingers tapped the glass of the skylight as he ducked down again quickly for fear of frightening their prisoner. Bobby had to climb on a chair to undo the catch. He was afraid of getting scratched, but the cat knew, and purred and rubbed himself against the boy's outstretched hand. As soon as the window was open his slim black body snaked between the bars and skittered down the passage.

Charlie and Jacques waited, motionless, leaning against the concrete retaining wall of the embankment. Belmont and Laurent were fifty yards further along the same dilapidated pathway which made a straight and narrow alley between the old houses and the steep slope of the motorway. Together they watched the cat come slinking along, delicately sniffing the snow, and then go trotting off towards the Rue du Général-Tuboeuf, the nearest opening from the narrow alley.

Belmont and Laurent were on duty there. They drew back in time for the cat to pass them on its way straight along beside the wall.

The hunt was soon up behind it. Flatfoot waved and the watchers, scooterized or no, roared down the parallel road to take their posts at the next intersections. Bobby ran to catch up with the others. They kept their prey in sight, the distance between lengthening or narrowing in accordance with the changing pace and sudden pauses of the black cat. The latter would sometimes slow down when he met another cat, halt to get his bearings, glancing distrustfully at a house, and would then set off unhesitatingly in the same direction.

'Where's the confounded creature taking us?' Charlie grumbled.

'One sure thing,' Belmont answered, 'we're not going to Belloy. I know the score . . .'

'If only he can keep it up!' Bobby sighed, an anxious eye upon his pet.

Far behind toiled Commissioner Sinet, his nose and moustache muffled in a warm scarf. He had trailed many an odd suspect in his time, but never had he seen so many on the track of a rat-snapper. The black cat never shifted from the straight course he was following and hardly paused to cross the roads leading into the centre of Puisay. After half-a-mile the Commissioner was frankly puzzled. He had memorized the general layout of the map and the route the cat was taking seemed to lead to nowhere. Beyond the Rungis road-bridge, over the lanes of the motorway, was a drab desert of factories, waste land and derelict warehouses. The Paris of tomorrow had not pushed its tentacles that far and it was hard to imagine a sky-scraper rising on that joyless horizon.

Ahead, the same anxiety gripped the investigators from the *P.S.N*. From time to time they would have to break into a sprint to keep in view the fugitive which would suddenly speed away from a group of passers-by, a growling dog or the threatening face of a scullery-maid.

'The black cat's taking us on a wild-goose chase,' Charlie was saying. 'If he goes straight on past the bridge we'll be in the police barracks. Talk about a surprise! We'll have frozen ourselves stiff for an hour seeing a police-cat home!'

'No,' Jacques said, 'he'll see he's gone wrong when he gets there. He'll turn left and come back into Puisay along the Rue d'Orléans.'

'The cat won't dare cross the main road.' Laurent gave his considered opinion. 'He won't go two yards before some Sunday motorist squashes him flat as a pancake. No, I bet he turns left, too.'

'He could turn round and jump into Bobby's arms as well, you know,' Belmont suggested.

Bobby was hunched forward, following the trail and suffering real pain to see it begin to be spotted with red. In the rearguard Commissioner Sinet plumped for the right, and the cat proved him correct as it turned unhesitatingly in that direction. Over the concrete arch that spanned the motorway went the whole gang, scooters and all. The boundary of Puisay passed through the middle of the bridge and both policeman and boys felt the difference when they crossed it.

Beyond was unknown country into which, close though it was, no one ever went. For the last five or six years the two adjacent suburbs, once joined by a network of friendly streets, had been cut off from one another by the bold sweep of the motorway as though they stood on opposite banks of a river linked only by the majestic bridge under which the main road traffic flowed day and night. Rungis was as distant as a foreign country both to Charlie and his friends and to Sinet, who had never set foot in it.

But the cat seemed to be on home ground, for his pace quickened. The hunt in its turn speeded up and soon the breathless foot-followers were outdistanced by their scooter-borne companions as they swept down a gloomy street bordered by warehouses.

At the end the setting sun was lost in the mists, and as the leaders came into the open they gave a shout. There, in front

of them at the end of a broad avenue which could be mistaken for the Boulevard Champaubert, stood the eight tower blocks of the Belloy Private Estate.

'It can't be! We must have gone round in a circle!' Charlie burst out and wiped his glasses.

'It can!' retorted Flatfoot. 'We're in Rungis. The bridge is behind us.'

Jacques and Laurent looked round in bewilderment. It took a long time for the truth to sink in.

'The buildings go up here twice as fast as they do in Puisay,' a mocking Belmont explained. 'You ought to get out a bit more. The suburbs round us are full of these beehives all put up to the same pattern by builders and architects in too much of a hurry.'

The buildings and the setting were exactly the same – on one side the bright lights of the new development and on the other a line of trees like the backdrop formed by the Parc de Sceaux.

'Watch out!' Bobby called. 'The black cat'll get away!'

They dashed across the snow-smothered gardens and through the covered car-park. The fugitive had slipped behind a group of Sunday strollers and in through the entrance to Block 6.

'I'll just go in with the Thiriets and Belmont,' Charlie decided. 'You others stay outside a moment . . . And keep your eyes open, see? The Hedgehog and his Duchess may well be sitting snug and warm behind one of those windows, watching their TV.'

Bobby went in first. He had a familiarity with the place bred elsewhere. The hall was as full of life as it was at the Belloy. There was the continuous hum of the lifts emptying and filling with suburbanites as well-dressed as their counter-parts in Puisay. The unfortunate black cat had nearly reached the end of his tether, but the warmth of the hall gave him a new lease of life. Unflagging he passed the staircase, disdained the basement door and headed straight down one of the corridors leading to the ground floor flats.

He slumped down on the mat in front of Flat No. 5 scratched the door and gave a heart-rending mew. His mistress was at home and she came out at once.

'Casimir!' she cried, raising her hands above her head. 'Here you are at last, my treasure! You've had Auntie so worried and poor Uncle's spent the last twelve days trying to find you in all the back alleys of Rungis. Where have you been, you naughty boy?'

She picked him up lovingly and hugged him. Then her eyes suddenly fell on the five boys standing silent and astonished in the gloom of the passage.

'Are you the ones who brought him back?'

'Casimir was in Puisay,' Charlie answered. 'All we did was see him safely home.'

'Don't hug him too tight,' Bobby added. 'Some idiot potted him with a .22 and the bullet's still inside him.'

Auntie's eyes widened in horror.

Her visitors seemed slightly disappointed and stared at her with embarrassing insistence. She was a plump little ball of a woman, dressed simply in black. Her fresh pink cheeks were surmounted by two bobs of fine white hair. In other words a typical cat-lover, the counterpart of old Madame Deuzy in Puisay. The Grand Duchess Natasha Popov had been a much more striking figure.

'Casimir didn't come by himself to Puisay, just for a change of scene,' Charlie went on. 'Someone stole him.'

'That's ridiculous! Casimir wouldn't fetch a thing in the animal market at the Porte Brancion. Some silly people think that black cats are unlucky.'

'We aren't superstitious,' Belmont laughed, 'but we all think quite a lot of people are soon going to be sorry Casimir ever crossed their paths . . . The funny thing was that before he made his getaway, the man who shot him took good care to remove the chain from round his neck . . .'

'Why?' Jacques asked. 'Did the disc have your name and address on it?'

The lady seemed very surprised.

'No,' she said, 'just the initials of the Society for the Protection of Animals, and a number. I must say that Casimir is a sort of orphan. They gave him to me, but I had to sign a whole lot of papers before they let me take him home with me. If you'd been lucky enough to have got hold of the disc, the Secretaries of the S.P.A. would have been only too happy to have given you my address. You'd have been here in an hour and poor Casimir would have been saved all this suffering.'

Charlie had stepped aside to search his pockets for a copy of the *P.S.N.* He opened it at the back page, folded it so as to show just the portraits of the Duchess and the Hedgehog, and waved it in front of Auntie's startled eyes.

'Please, have you seen these two people before?'

Behind him his friends held their breaths as they watched for the old lady's reactions. First she frowned and narrowed her eyes as she looked at the portraits. Then suddenly her face lit up.

'Of course, I know them well.' She was quite confident. 'Charming couple! He's on the Stock Exchange. Such a sensible man. I'm going to sell out my Four Per Cent to buy Porto Rican oil shares. I'll double my money in a year.'

'What name does he use these days?' The sly question came from Flatfoot who had just joined the group.

Auntie did not see the barb in the question.

'Vladimir Gorine. He and Natasha have rented one of the neighbour's flats for a month. I shall miss them terribly when they go.'

She pointed to the door opposite. With just the corridor

between them Jacques shivered as though an electric shock had passed through him.

'Really . . . That door over there?'

'Of course, Flat No. 7.'

Concealed behind the others were Belmont and Laurent.

'If we don't smoke them out,' they chuckled. 'Auntie's going to miss her Four Per Cents a darned sight more.'

The dear old lady quite misunderstood the boys' uncertainty.

'Come in! I'll give you such a tea-party as you'll remember for the rest of your lives.'

Jacques politely declined the invitation.

'Could we come another day? We're expected elsewhere. We've an important call to make nearby. But we're so glad we've seen Casimir safely home.'

One by one they sadly stroked the black cat and then they made off towards the hall. Before shutting her door Auntie shyly called after them, 'I should have loved to have given you something extra special . . . I do owe it to you.'

Casimir was cradled in her arms as Charlie turned with a broad grin.

'You've given us plenty already.'

11

The Hedgehog's gift to charity

THE caretaker's lodge was at the front of the building, just as it was at Belloy, looking out through a wide plate-glass window on to the comings and goings in the hall. The caretaker himself, a burly grey-haired individual, was oddly like a certain ex-policeman in a twelve-storey block in Puisay. Sinet asked him to switch off the main ceiling light so that he could lurk at the back of the room and see without being seen.

'Let the lads be, I'll go bail for their behaviour and that's more than you can say of a couple of birds you've got in the building.'

The puzzled caretaker was still looking at the portraits he had just identified as readily as the simple old lady of Flat No. 5.

'I can't get over it. The Gorines are only temporaries, but the neighbours can't say enough for that couple. I know she is a snooty piece and her husband looks a bit of a fool but they're quiet and they don't give me any trouble. Why, when Natasha gets me to pay off her taxi for her she always pays me back on the nail the next day – and she gives me a good tip, too.'

'She's playing the waiting game,' Sinet chuckled. 'Watch out when they start delivering Dior dresses for her! Your savings will go up in smoke and Natasha will be on her way, leaving you the receipt as a souvenir.'

He took the recent issues of the *P.S.N.* out of his pocket and slid them across the table.

'Read these. You'll soon see how and why Madame Michel lost her cat.'

He suddenly crouched in his chair as round the end of the corridor came the crafty half-dozen of the advance guard. Anxiously glancing over their shoulders, they held a vigorous council of war. Sinet could have set their minds at rest. Round the block twenty stout fellows resumed the watch they had kept two hours before on Number 33 Rue Mirandole. Casimir was safely inside, but someone else might want to get out. Indeed, although the boys did not belong to the Force, their police work was first-rate.

'You didn't ought to give them a free hand,' the caretaker grumbled.

'Why not? They won't go too far. They are decent, straightforward lads, not like the young roughs you read about in the crime reports. They've got might and right on their side, as well as a certain scorn for official procedure which I should be the last to disapprove of. To cut a long story short, they've got nothing to stop them, while at the moment, although I'm a police commissioner, I've not a thing I can use against the Gorines. I've no warrant for their arrest since we don't know their real names – and that's something crooks like them know how to take full advantage of. Of course I can always pick them up with the help of available witnesses. But what happens next? At midnight I've got to let them go, with a caution not to leave their domicile without my permission. If they're stupid enough not to make a getaway, I can put them inside for two or three weeks and then their lawyers'll kick up a fuss and get them out on bail. They'll do all they can to confuse the victims with counter-valuations, and the woman, who always plays the role of the innocent partner, will take the chance to vanish with the loot. When Gorine comes up in court he'll play stupid, snivel, pretend to be schizophrenic, mentally defective, deaf mute, cripple in a wheel chair – and repent all along the line. He'll get off with the lightest possible sentence. It'll do nobody any good and the victims can say good-bye to their savings. The courts can seldom enforce damages. So you can be pretty sure those boys have worked it all out already and have decided to get back what's owed to them by hook or by crook.'

In a few minutes the act was arranged and the parts allotted. Charlie took one last look round to make sure they would not be interrupted. There was enough activity in the entrance hall to mask the work of his commandos. The bulldog jaw of the caretaker had not appeared as yet and his lodge was in darkness. Outside, one of their friends who lived on the Belloy Private Estate had easily spotted all the fire escapes, tradesmen's entrances and other hidden exits. Five minutes before, sentries had been posted at these strategic points and the blockade was complete. The White Hedgehog could always try to break out, but he would not get very far. If he and the fair Natasha were at the cinema, an extra special welcome awaited his return to his lair in Rungis.

'Let's go,' said Charlie.

Without a sound they sped down the corridor. All was quiet in Flat No. 5. Auntie must have been killing the fatted calf in the kitchen for her prodigal cat. Uncle, however, had not returned and it was vital to dispose of the intruder if he put in an unwelcome appearance on the field of battle.

'Don't start a fight!' Flatfoot joked. 'The old boy's probably a good seventy. Just tell him his Casimir's come home and he'll run off to welcome him and leave us in peace.'

Cautiously Jacques approached Flat No. 7. He put his ear to the door and gestured to the others to keep quiet. An indistinct murmur came through the panel. Charlie had guessed correctly – there was the fruity voice of the TV announcer. Fly birds, the confidence tricksters lay discreetly low for a decent interval between their profitable sorties.

'They're in . . .'

Charlie took his place, carefully wiped his feet on the mat, raised his right hand and gave three soft and rapid knocks to lull the suspicions of those within. Half a minute later, when there had been no answer, he repeated his summons a little more loudly. The others were grouped in a semi-circle behind him, fiddling with gloves and scarves, smoothing their hair and screwing their faces into the forced smile of the door-to-door collector.

Inch by inch the door softly opened to reveal a man in a grey velvet smoking jacket. His short fair hair stuck out of his skull like a coat of prickles. He had small bright eyes, plump cheeks, a wide mouth, and short pointed jaw, a collection of characteristics vaguely suggesting the animal whose description the *P.S.N.* had faithfully circulated in all its five thousand copies.

'That's him,' Bobby hissed and dodged into the background.

The Hedgehog blinked short-sightedly and stared with grave suspicion at the delegation.

'You've got the wrong flat,' he said coldly.

There was the slightest trace of a foreign accent in his voice. Charlie exerted all his charm, bowed low and came up with a sickly smile on his face.

'We're selling raffle tickets for the Winter Holiday Fund,' he said, undismayed. 'Every year the charity sends five hundred boys and girls between the ages of eight and twelve for a fortnight's holiday in Savoy.'

The Hedgehog stiffened.

'Paris has had a foot of snow in the last forty-eight hours. The kids don't need to go looking for it hundreds of miles from Rungis and Plessis-Robinson when it's right there on their doorsteps.'

'It doesn't melt so soon in the mountains,' Charlie answered, still smiling. 'And the air is better up there . . . The tickets are only a franc each,' he added and stared at the ceiling.

Vladimir Gorine was about to slam the door when he noticed

the red, healthy faces of the group and suddenly changed his mind.

'Charity certainly looks as though it begins at home,' he said sarcastically. 'Why six of you to sell a raffle ticket?'

'Oh, it's a method we've perfected,' Charlie answered. 'Take it from us it pays off.'

Intrigued, the Hedgehog opened the door wider.

'A gimmick? Tell me a bit more about it.'

'It's no secret,' said Charlie, leaning gently up against the door jamb. 'Each one of us has a definite part to play in effecting a sale. It's sort of time and motion study applied to door-to-door collecting. What's more, our mass attack on a block of flats forces something out of those who are too mean or can't be bothered to give.'

'What's your job?' the Hedgehog asked him.

'I'm the patter man,' Charlie answered with a modest bow. 'Don't laugh! You nearly slammed the door in our faces, didn't you? It's open again now, isn't it? So you were taken in . . .'

Vladimir agreed. This gang of door-to-door collectors was beginning to amuse him. He pointed to the slender form of Bobby cowering behind his eldest brother.

'What about him?'

'He's the youngest and the best actor of all. His job is to soften up caretakers male or female. They all succumb to his innocent charm in five minutes. They let him in the front door and we pour in after him. If he finds a cat in the place his takings shoot up. He loves cats and they pay off well.'

The Hedgehog started slightly and his pink nose seemed to shrink a little. He passed on to the next, the burly Jacques, muffled up in a fleece-lined leather jacket.

'You can tell his job from the size of his shoulders,' Charlie went on. 'Somewhere we hit on a tough customer who has a few swear words or a clip on the ear to back his refusal. Our muscle man soon sorts things out. He's only got to show that ugly mug of his and we generally go off with the honours of war.'

Flatfoot waited with one arm folded, one hand dangling in a position reminiscent of a wounded bird. He made his own introduction.

'I'm the house-hunter, a kind of barometer of public generosity. We don't just operate any old where any old time. You have to wait until the end of the week or the end of the month when the family's in funds. You have to pick the right block in the street and go straight to the flat that gives the easiest. If they keep their ears open the others'll come running – they won't want to lose face with the neighbours.'

He pulled out of his pocket the dog-eared notebook he used as a reporter on the *P.S.N*.

'It's all down in here, even to estimated takings. I've only got to open it to let my friends know that the Agramon Private Estate at Rungis is a good place to try on a Sunday afternoon. Thanks to this information we're calling on you now.'

The Hedgehog was speechless. They gave him no chance to catch up.

'Well, are you going to give us something or aren't you?' Laurent fumbled in his patched old anorak as he raised the question. 'No one's forcing you to, and we're all too tactful to keep on at you. Your door's been marked by all the unsuccessful inquirers. You can decode it easily enough. A circle with line across it means a lady or gentleman who's always in the middle of something else. Two lines, that's the crafty so-and-so who never has any change. Three lines, that's the mean devil you can only get round by offering a discount. Four lines show the hopeless cases, people who are so mean and self-centred they won't give you a light if you ask for one and who hide their watches if you ask them the time. You can't get any worse than four lines!'

'Who are you?' The Hedgehog forced a laugh.

'The salesman. I give out the tickets and choose them deliberately and with due respect to the people we take the money from, even if it's only a franc.'

'And how many lines do you count on my door?'

'Four,' Laurent let fall in friendly fashion. 'But we haven't finished with you yet.'

Vladimir Gorine's pointed face went crimson with rage. These schoolboys with their sly and cynical methods of raising money for charity at once attracted and repelled him. One of them had still to speak. He stood a little apart. A lock of dark hair fell over his forehead and practically hid his eyes. He seemed to be staring into the flat and his left hand ceaselessly rattled a collection of small change.

'And you?' growled the Hedgehog.

'I'm the cashier,' Belmont answered sadly. 'All the efforts around me are concentrated in this pocket, which I'm afraid is never full enough. Distrust's the rule in any group, so I just look after the money, and the salesman tots up the balance sheet. If there's the smallest sum missing I get a beating up. My job's no picnic, I can tell you. One thing though, it has taught me early on that other people's money's sacred, that it stands for sweat and toil and that the worst sin is to spend it on your own selfish pleasure.'

Whereupon Laurent shamelessly produced a stained and crumpled ticket – and a losing one too, for the raffle had been drawn six months before.

'Would you like it?' he asked. 'Auntie took two. If you feel it's your lucky day, don't hesitate . . .'

'Maybe you'll win the first prize, it's a Mercedes 190,' said Charlie persuasively.

Belmont held out his hand. Beside him the muscleman looked pityingly down at the crook's sloping shoulders and pot belly. Flatfoot had his notebook out to take a written record of the customer's potential, while Bobby still dared not come forward but clenched his teeth to restrain his rage. He would have been only too happy to leap for the crook's throat.

Even a hardened con-man has moments of weakness which make him fall into the same state of mental blackout as his victims. All the same, the Hedgehog did not yield in the name of charity but only to the idea of paying cheaply for the amusing act these young idiots had put on for him.

'Good,' he said with a sneer. 'I'll take a ticket. Just one, but don't you come here again.'

12

The biter bit

VLADIMIR tiptoed across the drawing-room to find the price of his first and last generous act. When he turned round the coin nearly slipped through his fingers. These well-organized collectors had slipped into the hall and were watching him quietly and with the intense satisfaction of a hungry cat after a plump, defenceless mouse. Their bright eyes peered hither and thither inside the Hedgehog's cosy nest.

The spacious drawing-room was curtained in brocade. There were vivid Moroccan carpets on the floor. The close atmosphere was too stuffy for boys who had just tracked a black cat for a whole hour through the frosty air. The only light was from a lamp on a low polished mahogany table. Its ample shade cast a gentle rosy glow upon the shifting, dazzling figures of the twelve chorus girls prancing across the television screen.

The Grand Duchess Natasha Gorine reclined among the soft cushions on the sofa, in the attitude of the adventuress at her ease. As she watched the show, she puffed at a cigarette in a foot-long holder. Between Puisay and Rungis she had turned blonde and grown at least five or six years younger. An elegant green woollen dress covered her well-fed figure and set off the metallic grey of her eyes. She suddenly looked up and nearly swallowed her cigarette-holder to see her silent visitors standing there in the half light.

'What a silly joke, Vladimir,' she said wearily. 'I'd be very grateful if you'd clear these nasty little schoolboys out of our flat.'

At last the Hedgehog regained the use of his tongue and his face darkened angrily.

'Who said you could come in?'

'Nobody,' Charlie answered offhandedly. 'It's a privilege we sometimes take when the donor is so obviously well disposed. Our team had to work very hard indeed to sell you that ticket, but now we can guess how much a franc means to so poverty-stricken a household. And you can see how much we sympathize by the way we've all six come to your drawing-room like one man. Just take it as the tribute of a group of specialists who really know a thing or two about tight-fisted people!'

The White Hedgehog was acute enough to notice the threat beneath the bantering tone. Yet, on the surface, the intruders were behaving with exemplary and perfect politeness. There was something else below it, but what?

'Oh, I get it, you go around half a dozen strong to scare the mugs.'

'We're sure that's the last thing in the world you are,' said Laurent, 'and that our numbers didn't sway your choice.'

'You might have knocked,' the Grand Duchess angrily exclaimed. 'Oh do get rid of them, Vladimir!'

'The door was ajar,' Jacques pleaded. 'When a neighbour's cat pushed it right open we took it as an invitation and came in all together. You must know the cat, a black cat. It knows you well. It showed us the way in.'

Vladimir's hair could not have stood up more stiffly, and his roving eyes became still and glassy.

'A cat?' he said. 'Where did you see one?'

'We didn't actually see it,' Flatfoot explained. 'We only guessed that's what it was. It must be somewhere in the flat. Those creatures have no manners at all.'

Natasha Gorine leaped to her feet and bustled away to search the other rooms. Vladimir put an end to the joking.

'Take your money and clear out!'

He offered them the coin. Belmont took it respectfully while

Laurent handed the public benefactor his losing ticket. The Hedgehog thrust the piece of paper into his pocket without so much as a glance at it.

'Now hop it! Get out! The joke's gone on long enough!'

The six did not seem to have heard him, for not one of them moved. Belmont was examining the coin with religious zeal, weighing it in the hollow of his hand, turning it in all directions, flashing it in the light of the lamp and finally biting it, as if the nickel disc had been pure gold.

'Counterfeit?' Vladimir spoke sarcastically.

The con-man had made a stand in the middle of the room behind the low table with the lamp on it. Charlie and his men guessed he was beginning to be scared. Then Natasha came back, catless, her drawn face betraying her alarm. She hurried into another room.

'Your franc's okay,' Belmont admitted, 'it's only that one of us isn't quite happy about the price of the ticket. He thinks we should ask you for just a little bit more.'

He stepped aside to reveal someone who had been standing behind him until then. Suddenly Bobby and the White Hedgehog were face to face. The man did not immediately recognize the little boy whose hand he had held a fortnight before; in any case this final piece of haggling on the part of the cashier had made him furiously angry.

'I've given all I can! Beat it, or I'll get cross!'

Nobody took the slightest notice; on the contrary, the six boys imperceptibly closed in and their grinning faces came slowly into the pink circle of lamp light.

Belmont patiently returned to the attack.

'Bobby's right. Just suppose for a moment that you did win first prize – the Mercedes which must be worth twenty thousand francs at the very least. We'd be real fools to let you win all that and gain nothing at all ourselves.'

His off-hand assurance and the grins of complicity on his friends' faces intrigued the White Hedgehog more than somewhat. At every fresh suggestion he lost more and more ground.

'How do you mean?' he hissed.

The smallest of them piped up in his shrill treble.

'It's dead easy! Give us ten thousand francs cash and we'll fix it that your ticket wins. You'll have the car at half price and we'll be happy.'

The Hedgehog found himself back on familiar ground. He gave a great guffaw.

'But that's a racket!'

His mouth snapped shut at once while his flabby face went ashen grey.

The little boy from the Rue Mirandole was there, standing with his hands in his pockets, and in his sharp eyes was no longer the flicker of kindliness. What was more the others had closed in on him, too.

The Grand Duchess swept in again, still without the cat. Finding the gang firmly established in her drawing-room she flushed angrily.

'Vladimir! Get rid of these no-goods at once or I'll call the caretaker.'

Bobby's clarion call rooted her to the floor.

'Good evening, Madame Papadakis! So nice to see you again! I don't think this is such a nice flat as your one on the Belloy Private Estate.'

The two crooks soon recovered, but the shock had given them an ugly look and their malevolence thrived on this dangerous situation.

'What do you want?' the Hedgehog asked threateningly.

'My kid brother's just told you,' Jacques answered mockingly. 'We're sure you'll be on to a good thing if you give us ten thousand francs for this raffle ticket . . .'

'Even if you only win a tin opener,' added Flatfoot.

'Ten thousand francs!' Laurent repeated. 'That's not out of this world for a man like you. Just get used to the idea of opening your wallet and it'll all be so simple. It's only just four, so we've hours to spare.'

'Get out!' shouted the Hedgehog.

'When we've got the Thiriets' money back,' Charlie announced. 'And that won't take long.'

'Who are the Thiriets?' asked the other, playing innocent.

'Never heard of them!' stuttered the Grand Duchess. 'Not at Rungis, nor anywhere else.'

'Well, I can refresh your memories,' Charlie retorted.

Out of his pocket he drew a set of recent issues of the *P.S.N.* and fanned them out in front of the Gorines. Natasha hardly glanced at them as she pushed past Bobby and Laurent on the way to the door.

'I'm getting the caretaker: you'll laugh on the other side of your faces then.'

Jacques hurried ahead to open the door for her.

'We'd be awfully grateful,' he said with a low bow, 'if you'd ask him to ring the Police commissioner at Puisay. Monsieur

Sinet'll be over in ten minutes and then we can get down to brass tacks.'

The Grand Duchess whirled round and vanished into the other end of the flat leaving the Hedgehog to face his tormentors alone. Things seemed desperate, but Vladimir and Natasha had got out of trickier situations by a lighning change of address. If you have a guilty conscience you always keep your cases packed and an emergency exit open.

Natasha locked the door of her room, hurriedly slipped on the two fur coats belonging to Madame Papadakis and seized the heavy travelling bag which the two crooks used as their mobile strong-box. Vladimir would manage his own escape and they would meet again in a smart hotel near the Étoile in the heart of Paris, their rendezvous if ever they were forced to split up.

Night was falling and outside a light mist veiled the gardens and the car parks. Gently Natasha raised the window, sat on the sill and hauled the travelling bag up beside her. Now there was a bare three feet from her perch to the flower-beds below the ground floor flats. She was about to jump, when a figure stepped out from the wall.

'Can I give you a hand? Just pass me down the case, then I'll go on all fours in the snow and you can use my back as a step. Don't worry, you'll be all right.'

The boy who had addressed her wore a white crash helmet, red leather jacket, tight black jeans and cowboy boots. His mount chugged a few yards away in the car-park. Two other cowboys in the same get-up guarded the neighbouring windows and their sardonic smiles drove the Grand Duchess hastily back into her room with her strong-box. Quietly she closed the window, unlocked the door and tiptoed away to the far side of the flat. The back door would be as closely guarded, but there was another door from the kitchen to the service lift and thence directly down to the basement. It would be child's play then for her to make her escape via the underground garage.

Natasha carefully opened the door. Two burly duffle-coated figures, hoods pulled down over their eyes, blocked the entrance.

'Cooee!' one of them said softly.

She slammed the door and fled for the drawing-room. The others were still there in friendly conversation with Vladimir. Bobby's and Laurent's eyes bulged when they noticed that the mistress of the house had suddenly doubled her girth. Natasha sat clumsily down on the sofa, doing her best to hide her travelling case.

'Back so soon?' Flatfoot whispered. 'You can't have had a very long walk.'

She glared at him.

'Your friends are guarding all the doors and windows! You're a bunch of hooligans!'

'No one's stopping you going out,' Laurent protested. 'Take the loot for a little stroll. Wherever you go you'll always have a guard of honour at your heels. We've made up our minds not to lose sight of the ten thousand francs you picked up at Madame Papadakis's.'

'Hand it over!' Jacques insisted. 'That'll be the end of it and we can push off at once.'

The White Hedgehog began to wriggle on the hook.

'You're crazy! First of all, where shall we find that amount of money just like that? I can't summon up ten thousand francs at the snap of a finger.'

'My father found it all right!' Jacques growled. 'All he had to do was to go to the bank.'

'The banks are shut on Sundays. Wait till tomorrow.'

'I'd be very surprised if you trusted banks,' Belmont said. 'The good con-man keeps his cash where he can lay his hands on it.'

'Come on, try just that little bit.'

'Put your hand in the bran-tub and pull Monsieur Thiriet's money out. We won't look and see how much you've got left.'

'I haven't a thing,' growled the Hedgehog. 'If you don't believe me, search the flat.'

'We certainly won't do that. We've no right to make ourselves free of the flat, and anyway you don't own it. The police'll get on to it in the end and you don't suppose Commissioner Sinet'll wear kid gloves, do you? He'll sort you out.'

Vladimir realized there was no alternative to a refund. His visitors would never leave without taking what was owed them. It therefore remained to try to limit the damage.

'I split it fifty-fifty,' he said with an embarrassed air.

Charlie drew bow at a venture.

'Oh, of course! With the barber on the Place des Ormeaux, I suppose?'

The Hedgehog sagged and his silence spoke as loudly as an outright admission. Belmont was delighted to have been proved right. A bit of bluff cost nothing to break down the last line of defence.

'Fred and his nephew were put inside last night,' Charlie stated. 'So you've no need to share with those ham-fisted huntsmen. They backed the wrong horse when they had a shot at the black cat who brought us here. Casimir's doing fine, but if I were you I'd keep well away from him . . . you never know.'

A plaintive mew came from carpet level. Flatfoot and Laurent dropped flat on the floor to peer under the chairs in well simulated surprise.

The Grand Duchess shrank back on the couch wrapping her furs round her legs.

'Don't worry,' Charlie went on. 'You've cleaned this neighbourhood out and it's time you had a change of scene. If the police don't get you, I expect you'll find virgin soil in North Paris, with a barber or a waiter to take Monsieur Fred's place and point out the mugs for you to con. The dirty business'll always be a paying game for people like you, because it's easy to take advantage of the misfortunes and difficulties of others.'

'Now, pay up!' Jacques did not raise his voice.

At last the White Hedgehog got up from the Grand Duchess's side. Natasha swore like a trooper and hid her face in her hands as the travelling case was unzipped. Their opponents stood stiff and silent, all, that is, except the cashier who held out a demanding hand.

Vladimir turned, puffing with rage. He almost threw the bundle of notes in Belmont's face, but Jacques' icy glare stopped him in time. Bobby bent over like the hunch-back of Notre Dame while Belmont counted out the money, one note at a time, with due deliberation, on to his back.

'It's all there!' he announced and slid the bundle into his windcheater. 'Of course we'll keep the payment for the raffle, ticket in lieu of the one franc nominal costs and damages in the case. Well, that's the lot, so I'll be on my way.'

He reached the door, spent a long time wiping his feet on the carpet and then went out.

The others followed him, each with his last fling at the sick and angry crooks.

'I won't say good-bye,' Jacques said in his turn. 'Just keep away from us or it'll be the worse for you.'

Charlie did not forget the interests of the *P.S.N.*

'If you want to know what happens next, all you need do is buy a copy of our next issues, Tuesday and Friday, on sale at the Lycée Alfred-Jarry. I'm afraid we don't give free copies to future gaol-birds!'

Flatfoot stared at them a little longer through half-closed lids.

'I'm the artist,' he said pointing to the *P.S.N.* 'I couldn't have done a better job if I'd snapped you with my Rolleiflex ... A word of warning though. Better put a false nose on when you go out. There must be a good twenty thousand people looking for you in Puisay and Rungis.'

'Madame Deuzy's compliments,' Laurent chuckled. 'She's quite determined to give you a cup of tea one of these days.'

Bobby was the last to leave and all he said was '*Miaou!*'

For quite a while the Gorines sat and waited. The sputter of the motor scooters dying away in the distance completely reassured them. Yet, although the darkness which had just fallen favoured a rapid and discreet withdrawal, they began by slanging one another.

'You did the stupidest thing in your life when you ran into Madame Deuzy on the street corner,' the Hedgehog said bitterly. 'She may be eighty, but the old girl's got a better pair of legs and, what's more to the point, a better pair of eyes than you.'

'I'd have liked to have seen you in my shoes!' retorted the Duchess. 'Anyway this mess is all your fault. I needed a black cat to keep the old witch quiet, so what do you do? The best you can think of is pinching the neighbours' cat! We shouldn't have left him behind at the Belloy Private Estate.'

'It's easy for you to talk! The cat felt at home in the same surroundings. He'd have had me up and down between the eighth floor and the basement twenty or thirty times before I'd have been able to shove him back in his basket.'

'Then there was no point in telling Fred about it. That fool wrecked everything. Fancy sending his nephew to fire a rifle in a block of flats.'

'Nothing to do with me! Fred thinks himself the big shot, but he lost his nerve when he read the paper a kid had left in his saloon – that *P.S.N.*'

They peered through the curtains. All was quiet outside.

'Get on with the packing,' said the Hedgehog, 'and see you don't leave anything behind.'

He ventured out of the kitchen door. There was no one about. The service lift deposited him a moment later in the underground garage. The 404 had not been used since his last trip to Puisay. He found it in its place all right, but its four wheels had been removed and it stood on the concrete like a ship in dry dock. The saboteurs had left their signature. On each door-panel a cat's head had been daubed in white paint. Time was short, so Vladimir left the wreck and hurried back to the flat where Natasha was closing the last case. News of the fresh disaster did not depress her for an instant. When all is at stake, you must fight back fast against your bad luck.

'Quick, phone for a taxi! I'll look after the travelling bag, you take the heavy luggage along to the hall.'

They were about to leave the flat when the shrill ring of the door bell held them trembling. Then came a well remembered tap on the panels. The Hedgehog opened it cautiously. There on the threshold stood a pink-cheeked old man, with snow white hair, smiling as he cradled a fine black cat in his arms. The creature was purring happily. The Grand Duchess backed away in horror while the Hedgehog could hardly breathe for his sudden terror.

'I'd just bought this old puss to console Auntie,' Uncle cheerfully explained, 'but in the meantime our Casimir had come home and I don't know what to do with this one. Would you like him?'

Vladimir had to control his temper for fear of arousing the old man's suspicions.

'We're going away for four or five days. Yes, he is a lovely cat. Could you keep him and we'll think about it when we come back next week-end?'

Uncle seemed disappointed. Auntie hailed the fugitives from the opposite doorway.

'Don't forget my oil shares! I'm just waiting for you to tell me when, and I'll sell out my Four Per Cents.'

Away they went, hugging the wall like a couple of housebreakers. The White Hedgehog nearly dropped his heavy suitcases when he came to the end of the corridor and saw the hallway a blaze of light. There stood a silent group of about fifty people staring with hostile curiosity in his direction. The presence of this farewell committee was simply explained by the copies of the latest issues of the *P.S.N.* pinned up round the lifts. Luckily, beyond the gleaming glass doors, they could see their taxi waiting. The Grand Duchess, drooping beneath the weight of her fur coats, put her head down and swept on with the White Hedgehog following after, bruising his shins as the suitcases, heavily laden with assorted loot, bumped against them.

Outside, a thin scatter of snow had begun to fall from the murky sky and the thousand lights of the suburb flickered like stars through this filmy curtain. One man alone had the courtesy to come out to help the driver sling the luggage on to the roof-rack. He even opened the door for Natasha, handed her her strong box, helped Vladimir in and slammed the door behind him. Then he was so absent-minded as to get in next to the driver, who pulled away at top speed.

Too late the stricken Hedgehog realized what was happening.

'Where are we going?'

Commissioner Sinet, grandly confident, leaned over the back of his seat.

'I'm going to clip your wings, my lad, and this time it'll be for good and all . . .'

13

Happy Christmas

It was still too early to go home so Charlie threw a party for his friends in the editorial offices of the *P.S.N.* – the box-room of the Boulevard Champaubert. There were twenty-five in all, plus his sister Lily, and it took three gallons of grog and hot tea to thaw them out after the hardships of the afternoon. Then their appetites awoke and in one fell swoop they cleared the Barons' refrigerator until even the greediest could eat no more.

The appearance of a timid visitor recalled the merry-makers to their duties. Sitting on the witness sofa he assured them that he had some 'red-hot news'. This announcement provoked a howl of laughter which ran from one to another round the room with the speed of an electric current. For them the story had ended at Rungis in a ground-floor flat on the Agramon Private Estate, where the criminals had been unmasked, the stolen money returned and the black cat safely restored to its owners.

All that was left was to ring down the curtain. Undismayed, however, by the deafening mirth, the boy, a friend of Laurent Thiriet called Dauphin, told them eagerly. 'It's sensational! I've just met the Hedgehog and the Duchess.'

'Well what on earth are you doing in here?' growled Flat-foot. 'You should be after them, boy! Get back on their trail and don't lose them.'

'Not worth the bother!' the other replied blandly. 'I've just seen them get out a taxi at the top of the Avenue de Paris . . .'

'Where did they go?'

'Not very far – across the pavement and into the police station. Their luggage went in after them and then Commissioner Sinet himself. Believe me, he was the only one who looked at all cheerful!'

Charlie smacked his forehead in annoyance.

'In under two hours we've let events overtake us. We must get back on the job. Tuesday's *P.S.N.* has got to go to press by eight o'clock tonight!'

'But if the Paris dailies spill the whole story in one issue,' Lily objected, 'we'll have nothing for our forthcoming numbers. Had you thought of that?'

'Of course I had, but the papers only ever get the obvious side of the story. The black cat, the Thiriets and one or two of us have an exclusive on the inside story – the meaty, moving story of the case. For a couple of weeks we'll stick pretty close to reality and fix it as we need. Then from issue to issue we'll change the lay-out, alter the facts, twist the plot as we like, gradually sink our dear readers to the level of fiction and *The clue of the black cat* will end as it began – a "real-life" detective thriller!'

'You aren't afraid circulation will drop once the black cat disappears from the pages of the *P.S.N.*?' Flatfoot inquired anxiously.

Charlie brought his fist slamming down on the desk.

'We've done it once and we can do it again now we know what our readers really like. When we've finished with the black cat, you'll just have to find us another animal. It doesn't matter if it's a horse, a dog, a sheep, piglet, canary or fish, the great thing is to bring it into a story and to keep it there until the readers have had enough.'

Bobby was sitting beside his brother. He suddenly began to look thoughtful.

'Are you all right?' Lily asked him.

'Fine! I'd just remembered that mule last week . . .'

'A mule? Really?' Charlie pricked up his ears. 'Tell us all about it.'

'You know as well as I do.' Bobby scratched his head. 'The other night there was this mule strolling along the motorway between Arcueil and Villejuif while the cars were whizzing past at over a hundred . . .'

'Well?'

'A couple of flying squad men spent over an hour trying to clear him off, but the old mule gave them the slip on the lay-by whenever he wanted. In the end the poor old thing got himself run over down by the Chevilly bridge. Where had he come from? Where was he going? Nobody knows, and needless to say his owner's keeping mum.'

'But that's just splendid,' Charlie cried and begain scribbling away on a fresh sheet of paper. 'Let's see: *Southern Motorway gets mule!* . . . No, let's try again. *A mule on the motorway!* There's an odd contradiction in that headline that'll jerk the dullest reader awake . . . Bobby, my dear chap, you've got the makings of a first-rate journalist! Listen! The rest of us'll buckle down to writing the rest of twenty-five instalments of the black cat as advertised. Starting this evening you'll work every spare moment on this mule story for me. I want another black cat!'

'You'll get one!' Bobby shouted. 'The family owes it to you! Count on us three. I don't know yet where this mule will take us but it'll repay all the school and the *P.S.N.* have done for us.'

The Rue Mirandole slumbered under a blanket of snow and the doorway of Number 33 gaped like an oven in the smoky whiteness. The joyful spirit of Christmas was abroad in such strength that it seemed to be creeping from house to house even along this outcast street. Belle and her mother had had tears in their eyes when they saw Jacques undo his leather jacket and miraculously produce the bundle of notes which they thought had gone for ever. George Thiriet had yet to return from the laboratories at Bagneaux.

Hurriedly they disinterred from their boxes the somewhat tarnished decorations that had survived bygone Christmasses. Once again the magic of stars and balls and paper-chains transformed the slum flat, and disguised its cramping walls.

'How shall we tell him?' Sophie asked the children.

'Nobody must say a word,' Jacques answered. 'Father knows us all. He'll only have to see the smiles on our faces to guess. You don't fall on your feet like this every day of the week: lose all and then get it all back in a few days, thanks to a host of devoted helpers created by one evil-minded person.'

The collapsible table was laid for Christmas dinner. As a precautionary measure they had balanced one end on the backs of two chairs set at a safe distance from the door. The only present on this memorable occasion was in the place laid for the master of the house. It had been wrapped in gilded paper and tied with coloured ribbon, and a sprig of holly slipped under the bow had increased its value tenfold.

'I hope Daddy won't be able to guess,' said Bobby. 'What's more likely than he'll come in dead beat. No one'll say a word and he won't see his present until he sits down at the table. That's what I'm waiting for – the look on his face when he unwraps the parcel and finds the money!'

'Then he'll cry like a fountain.' Laurent's face was a picture of gloom. 'Granted he's got every reason to, but once he starts we'll all waste half an hour hugging one another and patting one another on the back while the chicken roasts to cinders. No! Take my word for it, let him have the good news as soon as his head comes round the door. Ma will only need to have a glass of brandy ready. He'll open the door to a chorus: 'Hurrah! We've got your ten thousand francs back! It's a great life! Sit down and have a drink, Father dear!" In other words, strangle sentiment at birth: that's what we need to do.'

'Each of you is right in his own way,' said Sophie. 'Whatever happens your father won't disappoint you. He can only give, particularly where his own family is concerned.'

'He was a bit too generous in the Papadakis' flat.' Belle laughed.

Bobby seemed to be looking for something, his mind wandering.

'Pity the black cat can't be in the party! He'd have deserved a nice fresh herring.'

Someone stamped the snow off his shoes outside. Firm footsteps rang on the tiles of the corridor.

'Here he comes,' hissed Belle.

Each took up his place. Sophie quickly lit the candles on the table. The master's fist rapped insistently on the door.

'Here I am! Let me in!'

Jacques unbolted it and pushed it open. George Thiriet came into the doorway, powdered with snow like Father Christmas, and stood there while he carefully removed his glasses and wiped them, almost as a reflex action. His pale grey eyes blinked short-sightedly and failed to focus. No one dared to say a word as they waited for him to cry out in surprise. He was blind to the radiant smiles of his family, the flat transformed, the table gaily decorated, his present in its midst – nothing happened as they had expected. His face was flushed and he seemed to be fighting for breath. His mouth opened and shut several times before he could get a sound out of it.

'I've . . . I've . . . I've,' he stuttered as he replaced his glasses.

He suddenly noticed the decorations and the happy faces. He came into the room swaying with joy.

'So you guessed! I was sure you'd have some presentiment . . .'

The others stared at one another in bewilderment.

'I've . . . I've found a wonderful flat!' he cried, raising his arms. 'I really have!'

Sophie and the children burst out laughing. This must be the hundred and first time in the last five years that he had promised them a marvellous move, including the return ticket to Madame Papadakis' flat that had almost cost them so much.

'But it's true,' screamed a despairing George. 'Prochimac have just bought two floors in a brand new block on the Place Brémontier. The management gave me priority on a four-roomed flat. We're moving in on Thursday. You've got to believe me! Put on your coats and come and see our dream flat! It's all ours . . .'

This time they did believe him, for the poor man was on the verge of tears. Sophie made him swallow a medicinal glass of brandy and Bobby expressed the good wishes of them all as he picked up the plate with the gilt-wrapped parcel on it, handed it to his father and murmured,

'Happy Christmas!'

As Bobby was coming out of school one evening he was astonished to be handed a summons by the caretaker. He had nothing on his conscience so, parting from his elder brothers, he whistled as he made his way towards the police station. There he was evidently expected, for the gendarme on duty showed him straight up without bothering to come with him.

Commissioner Sinet was peacefully puffing at his pipe in the big first-floor office and thumbing through the previous Tuesday's edition of the *P.S.N.*

'Nice to see you again,' he said, releasing a large cloud of smoke. 'Sit down and let's have a chat . . . You know your father has withdrawn his charge?'

'He had to,' said Bobby. 'In all honesty. The Hedgehog has paid all the money back.'

'Yes, but under what pressure?'

'None at all! My pals were able to do it all through kindness. We can't help it if Vladimir's a sensitive soul. He seemed to have quite a thing about the black cat.'

'Your Hedgehog won't be out of prison yet awhile. His arrest brought in a couple of dozen fresh charges which will make things tough for him. I'll eat my hat if he gets under five years. The Grand Duchess will get the same.'

'What about Fred?'

'He's in prison, too, and so's his nephew. The barber's shop on the Place des Ormeaux won't be open for a long time yet. It covered a lot of other rackets, some a lot worse than confidence tricks.'

He stopped talking to puff at his pipe and his silence seemed to invite a question.

'Any news of the black cat?' Bobby asked with a grin.

Sinet's eyes narrowed.

'Which one?'

'I meant Casimir. Toddles is just an ornament in the Papadakis' flat.'

The Commissioner answered with a laugh.

'Casimir's as fit as a fiddle now. Cats are queer creatures. A boot in the rump would have done more damage than that .22 bullet. I never believed these stories of cats travelling hundreds of miles over hill and dale to get back to a good master. I changed my mind that Sunday afternoon when I saw our black cat clawing his way home through the snow.'

'Was he really doing that?' Bobby ventured.

Sinet shrugged.

'Don't credit him with your feelings of vengeance. Throughout the case you've played his part. You've made him act and talk as you wanted him to. Casimir's really a peaceful creature who, all unknowing, has suffered because of the stupidity of a gang of crooks.'

He took refuge in silence once more, closed both his eyes and then opened the left one again to stare at Bobby, sitting good as gold on the other side of the desk.

'I've got a nice present for you . . .'

Bobby protested modestly.

'Surely I don't deserve it? We'd have never drawn the joker from the pack – Daddy's ten thousand francs – without you.'

The Commissioner put down his pipe and made as if to catch the *P.S.N.* which had fallen off the edge of his desk. To his amazement Bobby saw a fine black cat sitting curled up on Sinet's lap.

'He's yours,' said the Great White Chief of Puisay. 'I can't keep him any longer. He stops me going to sleep. He's so affectionate he gets on my nerves and he purrs all night like a steam engine.'

Bobby got up to have a closer look at the monster. It was not Casimir.

'What's his name?'

'I don't know. It's the cat that Uncle, thinking he was doing the right thing, was bringing home to Auntie at the very moment that Casimir regained his native hearth. They very sweetly gave him to me, and I took him out of the kindness of my heart. I'm passing him on to you in the hope that you won't be too hard on the confounded purrer. Take him away! His basket's on my hat stand.'

It was an order.

Unenthusiastically Bobby took his leave carrying the steam engine in its basket. In a well-chosen compliment Sinet expressed this hanks.

'The *P.S.N.*'s the tops! Tell your friends I said so. I hope they'll find something as exciting to follow up the black cat. In case of difficulty, I'll be only too happy to help . . . It'll be a pleasure.'

Bobby gave him a beaming smile.

'I'm busy working on the story of the mule with Charlie and Flatfoot.'

Sinet started, and the pipe fell out of his mouth.

'A mule now? . . . You must be quite crazy.'

Then another thought struck him and he looked at Bobby out of the corner of his eye.

'Not the mule on the Southern Motorway?'

'That's the one!' said Bobby. 'It looks as though he'll lead us quite a dance.'

The Commissioner stood up behind his desk and rubbed his hands.

'Splendid! Come round and see me at the same time to-morrow night. I'll have the flying squad reports and we'll work on the case together . . .'

These are other Knight Books

Paul Berna

THRESHOLD OF THE STARS

Young Michael Jousse's account of a momentous year on a research station in France, during which plans are made for a landing on the moon. It is a story of hopes and fears, success and disaster, with all the time sinister signs of sabotage and spies.

Henry Treece

HOUNDS OF THE KING

1066 – the field of what is now called Hastings. The Hounds of the King, Harold's personal warriors, gather for the last time to protect their king against the Normans.
One of these warriors is Beonorth, and this book is about his life in Harold's service. It is a story of heroism and adventure, and a magnificent picture of Saxon England.

These are other Knight Books

Richard Armstrong

SEA CHANGE

This outstanding sea story for boys was awarded the Carnegie Medal in the United Kingdom in 1948.
Cam Renton first went to sea when he was just fifteen, intending to work his way up until he was in command of his own ship. He started full of enthusiasm, but, after one year, he felt that he was no nearer his goal. It finally took something very like mutiny, and also a dangerous sea rescue, to prove to him that efficiency and training are all important. Richard Armstrong's aim in this book is 'to give a factual picture of life as it comes at a boy in the Merchant Service'. He himself went to sea when he was sixteen, and for many years sailed in liners, tramp steamers, colliers and tankers.

These are other Knight Books

Falcon Travis

CAMPING AND HIKING

This is a new book – written, designed and illustrated to be a guide for anyone who is going camping or hiking, whether alone, with a few friends, or in a larger party.
From equipment and personal gear to striking camp and packing up at the end, there is something of interest to everyone, however experienced they are.
The extra material covers many vital and fascinating aspects of life in the country – maps and compasses, knives and axes, first aid, logs and nature diaries, weather and safety precautions.
The book is published with the support and approval of the Scout Association, and covers almost all the tests for the Scout Standard and Advanced Scout Standard.
